The
Bare Essentials
of Investing
Teaching the Horse to Talk

The
Bare Essentials
of Investing
Teaching the Horse to Talk

Harold Bierman, Jr.
Cornell University, USA

 **World Scientific**

NEW JERSEY · LONDON · SINGAPORE · BEIJING · SHANGHAI · HONG KONG · TAIPEI · CHENNAI

Published by

World Scientific Publishing Co. Pte. Ltd.

5 Toh Tuck Link, Singapore 596224

USA office: 27 Warren Street, Suite 401-402, Hackensack, NJ 07601

UK office: 57 Shelton Street, Covent Garden, London WC2H 9HE

Library of Congress Cataloging-in-Publication Data
Bierman, Harold
 The bare essentials of investing : teaching the horse to talk / Harold Bierman, Jr.
  p. cm.
 Includes bibliographical references and index.
 ISBN-13 978-981-270-540-2 (pbk.) -- ISBN-10 981-270-540-6 (pbk.)
  1. Investments. 2. Finance, Personal.

 HG4521.B46 2006
 332.024'01--dc22

2006050086

British Library Cataloguing-in-Publication Data
A catalogue record for this book is available from the British Library.

Copyright © 2007 by World Scientific Publishing Co. Pte. Ltd.

All rights reserved. This book, or parts thereof, may not be reproduced in any form or by any means, electronic or mechanical, including photocopying, recording or any information storage and retrieval system now known or to be invented, without written permission from the Publisher.

For photocopying of material in this volume, please pay a copying fee through the Copyright Clearance Center, Inc., 222 Rosewood Drive, Danvers, MA 01923, USA. In this case permission to photocopy is not required from the publisher.

Typeset by Stallion Press
Email: enquiries@stallionpress.com

Printed in Singapore.

Preface

The objective of this book is to help an individual (or family) design a personal investment strategy. The optimum investment decision for you depends on your investment objectives and your current economic status, but it is important that you understand the investment alternatives. It is the premise of the book that the U.S. stock market has never been too high compared to the long-term value of its securities. It always pays to have some common stock in your portfolio. You should make your investment decisions given this fact (or this "claim" if you do not believe the analysis to follow). This book assumes that you are interested both in the return you are likely to earn from your investment and the risk of not earning the return target. It also assumes you are willing to give up the possibility of some expected return in exchange for some reduction in risk.

Most of the chapters have a very small amount of arithmetic. A reader can skip the arithmetic and still understand the major arguments being made. A better strategy is to read the book and not worry about the fact that a few sections are somewhat complex. The conclusions are easily understood.

A reader who is looking for a sure-fire (no risk) system for beating the market and becoming rich should look elsewhere. In fact, that person should seek a different world in which to live. While the book does offer a strategy for using the stock market for making a large fortune from a small investment, it recommends in its stead an approach to be used to increase the probability of earning a reasonable return on your investment. Why not choose the path to a fortune? I do not have an objection to wealth, but rather a natural desire for survival leads to the more modest earnings objective. Extreme strategies also have extreme risk. The objective is to be efficient in the application of a strategy leading to a good return rather than to be greedy in seeking an elusive pot of gold.

Avoiding investment in stocks because the market is too high has always been a bad long-term investment strategy in the U.S. Assuming the future performance of the market will be similar to the past, one should own some common stocks.

The focus of this book is "personal" investing since investing very large amounts of money leads to different strategy recommendations (if the policies of the firm being purchased can be influenced).

Chapter 1 of this book says that there are three essential rules. Why not learn the three rules rather than buy and read the entire book? The short answer is "that the devil is in the details". For example, one rule is to take taxes into consideration. But what does this mean if you have the choice between investing in stock or bonds? Detailed analysis is needed.

An Explanation of the Book Title

The Bare Essentials of Investing: Teaching the Horse to Talk

We all know that no one has ever taught a horse to talk. It is very unlikely that anyone will ever do so. But, see the story told in Chapter 1.

The author of this book believes that it is equally unlikely that someone will write a book that describes an investment strategy that will consistently beat the returns offered by investing in a diversified market portfolio.

This does not mean that some investors will not win (beat the market). Given the large number of investors, this is very likely. What is unlikely is that the investors' strategies can be written up and be effectively replicated.

I would have preferred to use the title "Where Are the Customers' Yachts?" But Fred Schwed, Jr. published that classic book in 1940 (Simon and Schuster).

Acknowledgments

My support aide, Barb Drake, has been invaluable for this and many other projects.

My wife was a good sport and despite her natural inclination to prefer English literature, read the entire book and offered numerous suggestions aimed at clarification of the concepts.

Jerry Hass, my colleague and friend, was always helpful.

Harold Bierman, Jr.
Ithaca, New York

Contents

Chapter 1

Three Basic Rules

There is an infinite number of different investment strategies available to investors. Some books advocate specific investment strategies that promise greater riches than they can deliver. But the reader finds out the goals are unattainable long after the books are purchased. There was a book published in 1987 that forecasted the depression of 1990. It sold 400,000 copies in 1987. The author was completely wrong and earned well over $1,000,000 prior to 1990. If he had been correct he would have earned many millions more.

The primary objectives of this book are to recommend some basic investment strategies and to give some insights as to the characteristics of different investment securities. It is assumed the investors are interested in keeping the probability of winning at a relatively high level but are willing to accept some risk. Some expected return is given up in order to keep the risk at an acceptable level. The basic investment recommendations are conservative. This is not the desired objective of all investors, and if the investor's objectives are different all is not lost. Enroute to our specific recommendations we will point out alternative strategies for different objectives. We will not recommend that an investor follow a strategy that has a small probability of a very large gain and a large probability of a large loss, but we will describe such a strategy.

We can not describe a strategy that is certain to lead to very large gains and little risk relative to alternatives because such a strategy does not exist. If we did have such a magical strategy we would sell it. The investors employing the strategy would drive the price of the securities involved up and their return down to a normal return.

Different investors have different attitudes towards risk and they will accept different amounts of risk and will aim for different expected returns. There is no one investment strategy that is correct for all investors.

When a strategy is recommended in the following pages the reason for the recommendation will be explained so that the reader may judge the reasonableness of the suggestion. No sure-fire rules for achieving large riches with no risk will be offered because these rules do not exist. The best we can offer is a strategy leading to a small probability of large losses. Unfortunately, a probability of losing does exist. There are no securities in the U.S. that guarantee that you will be better off at the end of the period compared to investing in alternative securities.

Three Basic Rules

The chapter title promises three basic rules for investing. They are:

1. Diversify;
2. Take the tax implications of your investment decisions into consideration; and
3. Market turns occur but they are difficult to predict.

The book will expand on each rule but let us consider the rule that one should diversify. If the investor's objective is to earn a higher return than all other investors, then the investor should not diversify. The best strategy to beat the performance of a large number of other investors is to invest in one common stock security (or better yet buy call options; a call option is a derivative to buy the security). This strategy is very risky, but offers a probability of beating the other investors. For most of us, the investment objective is to earn a reasonable return with a reasonable probability (a sensible amount of risk). A diversified portfolio is the best way to achieve this objective.

Three Real Life Stories

One title considered for this book was "An Investment Strategy for One's Heir." It is a title with considerable merit. If we consider a strategy to be used by our heir, then we bypass the problems associated with the fact that we think that we know how to beat the market, but we would not want our heirs to follow the same strategy because we know they cannot beat the market without considerable risk.

Bad investment strategies are found in a variety of forms. Consider the senior business officer of a major corporation who died ten years after retirement. At time of death her medium-sized estate consisted of the normal real assets (house, car, etc.) a large bank account, and many shares of the common stock of the company for which she had worked. She should have diversified her stock holdings to reduce risk.

A second story involves a nice elderly woman in her eighties barely surviving on a stock portfolio left to her by her reasonably successful husband. The portfolio was the result of a series of hunches of her husband and included 20 different securities including many of the faddish growth stocks popular during boom periods. Some of the stocks were paying zero or very low dividends. She needs to switch from growth stocks to dividend paying stocks so that she can pay her bills.

In both the situations described the strategies suggested in this book would lead to drastic changes in the portfolios. Do the strategies of this book always lead to improved results? Unfortunately, we cannot claim that degree of perfection, but they tend to improve the results.

The third story involves an executive not employing the strategies of this book who took all his savings and bought common stock of the firm that employed him. The company was a very small oil exploration company that then proceeded to be very successful in a string of drillings. The manager became a millionaire many times over. A careful reading of this book and following its advice is likely to have significantly reduced his winnings. Following the advice offered in this book will not necessarily lead to the best decisions, but it is very likely to beat the worst feasible decisions.

After the company found the oil, we know that the manager was correct in buying the firm's common stock. Before finding the oil it was far from obvious that the decision to buy a large amount of common stock in one very risky firm, where the manager was employed, was wise. The employees of Enron whose savings were invested in Enron common stock were not happy in December 2001.

Investment objectives change as one gets older. A young person might want to accumulate wealth. An old person might want the cash flow to sustain a lifestyle.

What are Our Objectives?

We want to define the nature of different securities and how to mix different securities into a portfolio that is consistent with the investor's objectives.

We will start with a basic discussion of the relevant factors to be considered and then discuss how to manipulate these factors to achieve the objectives.

The basic investment approach to be recommended in this book will strike many investors as being excessively conservative. This creates no great problem, if you object to any specific recommendations, hang in there and continue to read. You will be told how to invent your own strategy.

Throughout the book runs the conclusion that consistent with past history common stocks are a good investment, independent of the current level of the stock market. While the situation could change in the future, it is unlikely that there will be a time when the investor should ever be completely out of stocks. A mix of stocks and other securities is likely to be the suggested solution.

Some Basic Assumptions

There will be one very important assumption made throughout the book. We will assume that investors prefer higher returns to lower returns and less risk to more risk. This means that if two investments have the same risk it will be assumed that an investor will prefer the investment with the higher expected return. In like manner, if two investments have the same expected return, we will assume the investor will prefer the investment with the smaller amount of risk. We will call this type of behavior "risk aversion for the investor."

There are many real world examples, which contradict the risk aversion assumption. People do pay for the privilege of losing at the race tracks, do engage in state lotteries, and do play games at gambling casinos. Some people prefer more risk to less in these recreational situations, but we will stick with the assumption that people require a higher expected return before they willingly shift to a security with more risk.

A Fable

Many years ago in a far away country a wise old teacher was in trouble with his King. The King sentenced the teacher to death, but listened to the teacher's appeal.

The teacher pleaded for the King to give him five years in which to teach the King's horse to talk. The King liked to own unusual things and a talking horse would certainly be unusual and after considerable thought said "yes".

A friend of the teacher said to the teacher "Why did you make such a rash promise? You know no one has ever taught a horse to talk." The teacher said in reply: "Sometime before the end of five years:

1. The King might change his mind and pardon me.
2. The King might forget that he sentenced me to death.
3. The King might die. I might die.
4. I might teach the horse to talk.

In any event, I gain five years."

Note he did not promise to teach the horse to talk by next week. Why do I claim to know that the stock market is not too high from a long-term perspective? In order to prove that the market is too high from a long-term perspective you are going to need the earnings on stock over the next five, ten, 20, or more years. The financial history of the U.S. shows that common stocks have been a good long-term investment over the past 90 years. Of course, this does not prove they will be a good investment (compared to alternatives) in the future. That is why diversification is recommended.

Summary

This book will tell you how to make a reasonable return (per dollar of investment) over a long period of time with acceptable risk. If you want to earn vastly large earnings from investments in a relatively short time period, you should have an extremely large investment fund, or alternatively not follow the advice of this book.

To become vastly rich you will have to work hard, be lucky (e.g., strike oil) or marry well (financially as well as in other ways). If you have modest wealth, the strategies recommended in this book are not likely to lead to vast wealth as a result of your investment strategy, but they should help avoid poverty, and are likely to lead to reasonable wealth.

Questions

1. How does an investor diversify?
2. What activity leads to a lower expected return and considerable risk?
3. Assume a stock selling for $100 pays a $8 dividend. How much will the owner of one share net if:

   a. A zero tax rate
   b. A 0.35 tax rate
   c. A 0.65 tax rate
   d. A 0.15 tax rate

4. Name an investment that has zero risk.

Part I

Diversify

"Diversify Wisely"
Is one thing I've learned.
I may never get rich,
But I'll never get burned.

Florence M. Kelso

The first basic rule we will consider is "diversify." As part of this section, we will introduce stock valuation, consider alternative investment vehicles, and then proceed to the construction and evaluation of an investment portfolio. With the alternatives available to investors today, it is relatively easy and inexpensive to diversify.

Chapter 2

The Expected Return

What return can you expect to earn on an investment? Investors are very much interested in the return they have earned on investments in the past and the return they can expect to earn on prospective investments. The concept of return on investment is a growth concept. If a $100 investment grows to $110 in one year, we say that the investment earned a 0.10 annual return on the original investment. If the investment grows to $121 in two years, it is again a 0.10 annual return even though the investment earned a total of $21 or 0.21 in total on an original investment of $100 over a period of two years. The fact that it took two years to earn the $21 is significant in computing the return. The $21 of income on an initial investment of $100 for two years is an example of compound interest of 0.10 per year and a 0.10 annual return.

The power of compound interest is tremendous when interest rates are high and time periods are long. For example, if the interest rate is 0.25 per year, an investment of $1.00 will grow to $1.25 after one year. The $1 will grow to $9.31 over a ten-year period and at the end of 80 years the $1 earning 0.25 per year will be worth $56,597,994. We can say that $1.00 invested today that will pay $56,597,994 in 80 years will earn 0.25 per year. The return on investment concept as defined in this chapter is the crux of investment practice.

The general formula being applied in the above example is $(1 + r)^n$ where r is the annual interest rate of 0.25 and n, the exponent, is the number of years for the accumulation. The compound interest term $(1+r)^n$ is called the accumulation factor. If the initial sum invested is multiplied by the accumulation factor, we obtain the future value of the investment. Table 1 gives some illustrations of the power of compound interest for different interest rates (r) and different time periods (n). Present or future values

Table 1.   The Future Value of $1 $(1+r)^n$

Number of Periods	$r = 0.10$	$r = 0.25$	$r = 0.30$
1	1.10	1.25	1.30
10	2.59	9.31	13.79
80	$2,048.40	$56,697,994.00	$130,450,000.00

are very sensitive to the choice of the interest rate. Appendix 1 shows the basic derivation of two compound interest formulas.

Economists and finance people speak of the annual return earned by an investment as being the internal rate of return of the investment. It is both the annual growth rate of the investment as well as the highest rate at which funds can be borrowed to repay a loan to buy the investment if the cash generated by the investment is used to repay the loan. An investment of $100 that is expected to return $121 at time 2 has an internal rate of return of 0.10. The investor can borrow $100 and pay 0.10 interest ($21) at time 2 using the investment proceeds of $121 to pay the interest and principal of the debt.

We will next illustrate the return on an investment using one time period for two reasons. For one thing, the computations are easier than for several time periods and secondly, for most personal investment purposes, it is the most useful measure of return.

Assume a common stock is selling for $100 and the investor expects to receive one year from now a dividend of $2 and expects that the stock price will be $112. The return on investment is:

$$\text{Return on investment} = \frac{(112 - 100) + 2}{100} = \frac{14}{100} = 0.14$$

or more generally,

$$\text{Return on investment} = \frac{\text{Price Change} + \text{Dividend}}{\text{Price Now}}.$$

The investor expects to earn a 0.14 annual return on the investment. Obviously, forecasting the stock price one year from now is not likely to be an easy task. An estimate of the expected stock price will have to be made to compute the expected return on a common stock investment. The above calculation is sometimes called the "total return" as distinguished from the "dividend yield" of a stock which in the above example is 2%. The investor has two benefits, cash dividends and stock price increase.

Some securities (e.g., some preferred stock) promise a constant flow of dividends (subject to the firm's ability to pay them) and the calculation of the return is more simple than the above calculation, if we do not expect the stock price to change. If the stock price is not expected to change, then we have:

$$\text{Return on investment} = \frac{\text{Dividend}}{\text{Price Now}}$$

for the return of a common or preferred stock issue with no expected stock price change. This is also the dividend yield. For example, if the dividend is \$8 per year and the current stock price is \$100, the investor in the stock can expect to earn 0.08:

$$\text{Return on investment} = \frac{8}{100} = 0.08.$$

The dividend yield is 8%.

If the cash flows from the investment last longer than one period but are not a perpetuity (do not continue forever), or are not the same each period, then the best method of finding the internal rate of return may be by trial and error. For example, assume an investment costing \$160 will earn \$104 at time 1 and \$92 at time 2. The $104 + 92 = 196$ of cash flows consists of dividends, return of the \$160 cost and capital gains. What return on investment will the investor earn? Assume we try a trial and error approach with our first estimate of the internal rate of return being 0.10.

The present value of the two future cash flows using $(1.10)^{-n}$ to accomplish the discounting is[1]:

Time		Present Value of Cash Flows
1	$104 \times (1.10)^{-1} =$	95
2	$92 \times (1.10)^{-2} =$	76
		\$171

The discount rate is the cost of the capital being used by the investor. What return do alternatives of comparable risk offer? For the discount rate to be equal to the internal rate of return, we need the present value of the

---

[1] A review of mathematics: $(1+r)^{-n} = \frac{1}{(1+r)^n}$ and $(1.1)^{-3} = \frac{1}{(1.1)^3} = \frac{1}{(1.1)(1.1)(1.1)}$.

benefits to be equal to the cost of the investment of $160. We need a higher rate of discount than 0.10. Using 0.20 for our second trial we obtain:

Time		Present Value
1	$104 \times (1.20)^{-1} =$	87
2	$92 \times (1.20)^{-2} =$	64
		$151

The 0.20 discount rate is too high since $151 of benefits is less than the $160 initial outlay. Now let us try 0.15 as the discount rate:

Time		Present Value
1	$104 \times (1.15)^{-1} =$	90.43
2	$92 \times (1.15)^{-2} =$	69.57
		$160.00

Using 0.15 the present value of the benefits is $160 and we conclude that the $160 investment is expected to earn 0.15. For example, if $160 grows at 0.15, at the end of one year the investor has $184 if the investor then takes $104 out of the investment there will be $80 remaining at time 1. The $80 will grow at a 0.15 rate to be $92 at time 2. Thus the investment has a 0.15 growth rate or more simply a 0.15 internal rate of return. The internal rate of return of an investment is an extremely important input in evaluating investment alternatives, but it must be used carefully or less than optimum decisions will be made.

For example, a very high rate of return for a very short period of time may not be as good an investment as the rate of return implies. Assume $1,000 can be invested to earn a 0.50 return. This is a very high return for a year. However, assume the period of the investment is for nine days or 1/40 of a year. The $1,000 will grow to $1,010.[2] The $10 earned on $1,000 is not that impressive. If the funds could have been invested to earn 0.50 for an entire year, the investor would have $1,500 at the end of the year. The high rate of return needs time to operate or the economic significance of the high return is greatly reduced.

The above example brings to the fore another investment complexity. After the passage of the nine days (1/40 of a year), at what rate will

---

[2] $1,000(1.50)^{1/40} = $1,010.

the funds be reinvested? The reinvestment rate becomes very important when we are considering alternatives that are competing with each other for scarce investment funds.

Assume that at the end of the nine days during which 0.50 is earned the funds can be reinvested to earn 0.10 for 39/40 of a year. At the end of the year, the investor will have $1,108.[3] If the investor can earn 0.11 on $1,000 for the entire year, at the end of the year the investment will be worth $1,110.

Thus, 0.11 for a year is better than 0.50 for 1/40 of a year and 0.10 for 39/40 of a year.

We are interested not only in the percentage return but also the period of the investment and the reinvestment opportunities when the period of high growth ends.

Risk

Up to this point in this chapter, we have implicitly assumed certainty exists. We also have to consider returns in the context of an uncertain world.

The first problem is that we have to determine the nature of the cash flow being considered. Assume there are two investments A and B with the following cash flows: A has an $1,000 outlay at time 0 and $1,200 benefits (positive cash flow) at time 1. B is expected to return $1,560 at time 1.

	Time 0	Time 1	Internal Rate of Return
A	−1,000	+1,200	0.20
B	−1,000	+1,560	0.56

Which investment would you prefer?

Most of us would prefer B. It is "clearly" superior to investment A. However, consider the fact that A is the basic cash flow of an equity investment earning an internal rate of return of 0.20. B is the cash that flows to the stockholders from financing ten units of A with $9,000 of debt costing 0.16, and $1,000 of equity. For ten units of A financed with

---

[3]$1,010(1.10)^{39/40} = $1,010(1.09738) = $1,108.

90% debt the cash flows are:

	Time 0	Time 1
A (Basic Investment Flows)	−1,000	+1,200
Debt (0.16)	+900	−1,044
Stock equity flows (A plus Debt) for A	−100	156
Stock equity flows (for ten units of A)	−1,000	1,560

With ten units of A each financed with $900 of debt and $100 of stock equity, we would have investment B. B is equivalent to ten units of A financed with $900 of 0.16 debt. With $900 of debt, only $100 of stock is needed for a $1,000 investment.

It is important to know whether we are investing in a high debt leveraged situation or in a straight investment. Consider a piece of real estate that requires an investment of $1,000 and will be worth $1,200 in one year. This is a 0.20 return. This real estate clearly can be presented as an investment yielding 0.56 to the equity participants if $900 of debt costing 0.16 is used in the analysis. If the deal for A can be replicated ten times, we have investment B. If the alternatives are merely described as two investments A and B, one yielding 0.20 and the other 0.56, this is misleading. The investment A might have a very small amount of risk. If A has a small amount of risk, B, the debt leveraged version of A, can still have a very large amount of risk because of the large amount of debt leverage. Thus, to evaluate any set of investment cash flows we have to know the nature of the investment, including the amount of debt implicit in the investment. The use of debt tends to increase the expected return and this is very attractive to investors. But the use of debt also increases the spread of outcomes and the probability of a loss.

The complexity of uncertainty can also appear when the security is itself debt. A triple A bond (the highest grade industrial debt security) may be yielding 0.09 while a double A bond (the next highest grade industrial debt security) is yielding 0.10. It might appear that an investor can earn a higher return investing in the double A bond yielding 0.10 than in the triple A bond.

In most cases, the return actually realized will be higher with double A bonds than with triple A bonds, but double A bonds will tend to go bad slightly more frequently than triple A bonds. It does not take many bad events of this type to cause the actual realized return from a portfolio of the double A bonds to equal or fall below the actual realized return from a portfolio of triple A bonds.

Both the 0.09 return from the triple A and the 0.10 return from the double A bond are based on contractual promises to pay principal and interest. Looking at a large number of bonds over a very long period of time, we would find that the actual return earned from both sets of bonds was below the 0.09 and 0.10 promised returns (abstracting from such complexities as call premiums and decreases in interest rates) because of payment defaults. We can expect double A bonds to default more frequently than the same dollar amount of triple A bonds. This does not mean that more risky bonds are not good investments. It does mean that the investor will earn a smaller return than the contractual rate of the risky bonds.

Thus, if securities promising different returns are being compared, the degree of risk associated with each security must be weighed before a final choice is made. We can expect securities promising higher returns to also have more likelihood of not being able to pay the promised returns.

Why Use Debt?

Debt is used with the objective of enhancing the investor's return. Assume the investor can borrow funds at 0.08 and can earn 0.12 on a basic investment. Assume the investment is $1,000 and the investor uses $900 of debt. The amount of interest paid at time 1 is 0.08(900) = $72 and the total amount paid is $972 at time 1.

| | **Time** | | **Return & Cost** |
	0	**1**	
Basic Investment	−1,000	1,120	0.12
Debt	+900	−972	0.08
Net of Debt	−100	+148	0.48

With the use of debt, the return on the investment described above is increased from 0.12 to 0.48.

Hedge funds and private equity both increase the returns they offer investors by the extensive use of debt.

If the basic investment actually earns 0.08 instead of 0.12, we have:

	Time		
	0	**1**	**Return & Cost**
Basic Investment	−1,000	1,072	0.072
Debt	+900	−972	0.08
Net of Debt	−100	+100	0.00

With these facts, the use of debt reduces the return actually earned from 0.072 to 0.00. The use of debt does not always work out as planned.

Returns and Taxes

Frequently in investment finance when we can recommend a definite course of action, we find that the recommendation is based on tax effects. In this section, we shall point out some of the choices and opportunities involving taxes. Consideration of taxes will be reviewed throughout this book. This is only an introduction.

A tax exempt security is an investment that should be considered as soon as your marginal tax reaches a given magnitude (the exact relevant rate will depend on the yields of taxable and non-taxable securities and the applicable tax rates). On $100,000 of income an investor pays $30,000 of tax, but for the last dollar earned and the next dollar earned (the marginal dollar of income) the tax may be 40% (the marginal tax). The marginal tax rate might increase further if the taxpayer earns enough to move into a high tax bracket (a higher tax rate).

Let us assume that taxable securities are yielding 0.12 and comparable risky tax exempts are yielding 0.10. We have an investor who is paying taxes at a marginal rate of 0.4. The after tax yield of a taxable security is:

$$0.12 - 0.12(0.4) = 0.072$$

or alternatively:

$$(1 - 0.4)0.12 = 0.072$$

which compares unfavorably with the tax exempt yield of 0.10. With these facts, an investor with a marginal tax rate (t) of 0.167 would be indifferent to the taxable and the tax exempt securities:

$$(1 - t)0.12 = 0.10$$
$$t = 0.167$$

Given the taxable yield of 0.12 and the tax exempt yield of 0.10, any investor with a tax rate in excess of 0.167 would prefer the tax exempts yielding 0.10 to taxable bonds yielding 0.12.

A second device for avoiding taxes is to have the income attributed to an individual paying a lower tax rate. If you have minor children you should consider making them a gift of securities (frequently the donor sets up a trust). If you intend to make a gift to your children at some stage in their lives, from a tax point of view making the gift early in their lives is sensible. While you cannot use the earnings to supply essentials, the funds that are accumulated could be used when the children are mature and no longer dependents. The low tax rates applied to their low incomes facilitates the accumulation of the earnings generated by the securities. The current tax laws should be consulted before acting.

The third technique is to buy common stocks that fit your tax profile. If you are a low tax rate person then high dividend yielding stocks are attractive. If you are in a high tax rate then the opportunity to defer paying taxes by buying stocks that are paying low or zero dividends and accumulating retained earnings (profitably reinvested) becomes more attractive. The choice of common stock (or other securities) should be a function of the investor's tax rate.

The buying of a stock of a firm that is heavily reinvesting is an example of deferring income taxes by the investor. An investor can defer the receipt of the income or can defer taxes by setting aside income that has been earned in an eligible retirement account (for example, either an IRA, 401 K, or Keough plan). These plans have the advantage of deferring the taxation on both the income earned and invested in the plans and the interest and dividends earned on the securities that are purchased.

The power of deferring the taxes can be seen by an example. Assume that 0.15 can be earned before tax, 0.099 after tax, and there is a 0.34 tax rate. The investor can defer taxes for ten years. We will assume the tax rate ten years from now will still be 0.34.

If the $100 is received now as a dividend, it will be taxed and the investor will have $66 after tax. The $66 will earn 0.099 after tax every year and after ten years the investor will have:

$$\$66(1.099)^{10} = \$169.64.$$

If the $100 is reinvested by the corporation to earn 0.15 and then the entire amount is taxed at a 0.34 rate, the amount accumulated will be:

$$(1 - 0.34)100(1.15)^{10} = \$267.$$

The value is almost doubled!

If ten years from today the investor expects to be paying taxes at a lower rate of 0.20, then the amount accumulated will have an after-tax value of:

$$(1 - 0.20)100(1.15)^{10} = \$324.$$

The advantages of tax deferral can be dramatic.

The fourth device to manage taxes includes the entire set of tax shelters. These alternatives are apt to be more risky than the devices described to this point. The tax shelter may be a real estate venture (in a sense your house is a tax shelter) but it is apt to be more unusual.

Several years ago the buying or leasing of boxcars was a popular tax shelter. Unfortunately, the boxcar owners found that they not only received tax deductions, but they also had unlimited liability for the demurrage charges (rent for parking the boxcars on the railroad's tracks) associated with their boxcars. It is well to realize that even if you are in a 0.40 tax bracket (federal and state), and every $1 of loss saves you $0.40 of tax, that if you lost $1 to get the deduction, you are out $0.60 on net.

Another popular form of tax shelter is the oil or gas exploration venture. Drilling oil wells have significant tax advantages. Unfortunately they also have a lot of risk. Other popular tax shelters are timber, fruit groves, cattle, and real estate.

Another tax strategy somewhat similar to tax shelters is to invest in collectibles, stamps, coins, art, diamonds, quilts, and the like. All these have the characteristic of having expected value increases, but these increases are not taxed until the item is sold (this assumes the gain is reported thus taxed). The ability to defer the tax is valuable. The problem with items of this type is that there is no guarantee that the value will increase or that they can be sold at a good price when cash is needed. At any given moment in time there is a wide gap between what you would have to pay to acquire the asset and what you would net out if you sold. If you are not an expert you might pay too much for the asset with the result that little or no gain is ever achieved.

Taxes also affect preference for bonds selling at face value or deep discount bonds (bonds selling at much less than face value), choice of taxable or tax exempt bonds, and by affecting their market yields, the choice between debt and preferred stock.

Summary

The expected return on investment is a basic concept. In this chapter we learn that there are complexities in evaluating the return expected to be earned by an alternative. The investor must be interested in the duration of the return (the life) as well as the amount of risk associated with the return. Since the relevant measure of rate of return is after all and any taxes, the tax law that is in effect during the life of the investment must be considered.

Today's stock price and the expected stock price one period from now are both important inputs to compute the stock's expected return. If stock prices are too high today, it is difficult (and may be impossible) to earn the required return. Thus, the level of the market is important to the making of good investment decisions.

Appendix 1

Compound Interest

Let,

X	be the initial sum
r	be the annual interest
n	be the number of years
FV	be future value
PV	be present value

$\underline{n = 1}$

$$FV = X + rX = X(1 + r)$$

$\underline{n = 2}$

$$FV = X(1 + r) + rX(1 + r) = X(1 + r)^2$$

For any year n

$$FV = X(1 + r)^n$$

The term $(1 + r)^n$ is the accumulation factor.
If we replace X with PV

$$FV = PV(1 + r)^n$$

and dividing by $(1 + r)^n$:

$$PV = \frac{FV}{(1 + r)^n} = FV(1 + r)^{-n}$$

The term $(1 + r)^{-n}$ is the present value factor. The present value (PV)
is FV times $(1 + r)^{-n}$.

Questions

1. An investment of $100 earns 0.10 per year for three years. At time 3, the investment's value will be $ _____.
2. If you have $133.10 at time 3, and assuming a 0.10 discount rate, the present value is $ _____.
3. A stock is now selling at $50 and is expected to sell at $56 in one year. It pays $2 a year dividend. What return will the investor expect to earn?
4. (Continue 3). What is the firm's dividend yield?
5. An investment has the following expected cash flows:

Time 0	Time 1	Internal Rate of Return
−1,000	+1,150	0.15

   Funds can be borrowed at 0.08. Assume zero taxes.

   If the investor borrows $800, what return will an investor buying the equity earn?
6. Taxable securities yield 0.10 and tax exempts yield 0.06.

   What is the tax rate that an investor must have to buy a tax exempt, if the investor wants to buy a debt security?

Chapter 3

Securities are a Fair Gamble

If you invest in any security, the ultimate outcome is uncertain. Even with a Federal Government security where the cash flows are certain there is uncertainty about the real value (inflation adjusted) of the payoffs from the security even though the dollar amount of the payoff is certain. With other securities, there is uncertainty about the amount to be received prior to maturity as well as the value that will result at maturity. This means that we are interested in the entire range of possible outcomes that can occur. We need summary measures of these outcomes that will enable us to evaluate different alternatives. This chapter will describe the use of several summary measures that can be used when there is uncertainty.

The first measure we will consider is the average return or as it is sometimes called the expected return. Consider a fortunate worker in the early nineteenth century in the state of Nevada who finds that he has $100 in gold. The gold could be invested in a bank, but assume the bank has a 0.2 probability of failing this year. Imagine placing two red and eight black balls in a jar and then randomly taking out a ball (no peeking allowed). If the ball is red your bank fails. Even if the ball is black you are not safe since the game is repeated again next year. With this magnitude of risk associated with banks a mattress might look relatively safe.

Assume the bank pays annual interest of 0.08. The investor putting $100 into the bank for one year has 0.8 probability of having $108 one year from now and 0.2 probability of having zero.

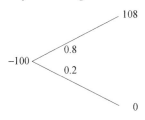

By definition, the expected monetary value of a gamble is equal to the sum of the product of each outcomes times the probability of the outcome. For our example, we can compute the expected value of placing $100 in the bank by multiplying each of the two outcomes by its probability and summing the products:

Outcome		**Probability**		**Expected Value**
108	×	0.8	=	$86.40
0	×	0.2	=	0
				$86.40

Next we have to deduct the $100 initial outlay from the expected value of the outcomes if the asset is undertaken to obtain the net expected value of the investment. The net expected value of the example is a negative $13.60. When the expected value is negative the investment is called an "unfair gamble". Normally a negative expected value leads to a rejection of the investment opportunity unless the gamble has entertainment value.

If we change the facts so that the bank deposit is insured by the Federal Government, now the investor receives back $108 with certainty and we have a "fair gamble". With a fair gamble, we receive an expected value that is equal to or greater than the initial outlay.

Assume a situation where you invest $100 and will immediately receive $250 if a coin is flipped and heads appear and $0 if tails appear. Both of the below decision trees illustrate the situation.

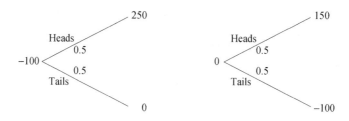

The right-hand figure differs from the left in that the $100 outlay has been subtracted from the outcome of each path. Using the right-hand picture, the expected value of the gamble is:

Outcome		Probability		Expected Value
$150	×	0.5	=	$75
−100	×	0.5	=	−50
		Expected Value		$25

The left-hand picture leads to the same expected value $(0.5 \times 250 - 100) = \$25$. The expected value is positive and we have a "fair gamble". If the investment earns $250, the percentage return is 150% and with $0 the return is minus 100%.

Just because an investment opportunity is a fair gamble does not mean one should accept the investment. But in making an investment decision it does help to know that the expected value is positive and that the gamble is fair. If the expected value is negative, we have an unfair gamble.

Most investors consider investment in conventional corporate securities to be fair gambles. A study of the history of returns indicates that on the average one earns something from investing in corporate securities. It does not mean that one cannot lose, but rather the transaction is a fair gamble in the sense that at the time of making the investment the expected value is positive (the determination of the probabilities of the outcomes is not as easy as in the above examples).

Means and Variances

We find it useful to define two statistical terms. Above we used the concept of expected value. The expected value is also called the mean or the average of the outcomes. Thus the terms average, mean, and expected value can all be used interchangeably.

When one outcome is a gain of $150 and the other outcome is a loss of $100 and if the two outcomes are equally likely, the mean of the probability distribution of outcomes is:

$150	×	0.5	=	$75
−100	×	0.5	=	−50
		Expected Value		$25

Note that with these facts the expected value is $25 but the actual outcome will be either a gain of $150 or a loss of $100. The expected value cannot occur.

In addition to the expected value an investor is also interested in the risk of the investment. The statistical measure "variance" is frequently used as an approximate measure of risk. The square root of the variance is also widely used. It is called the standard deviation.

The variance is a measure of spread of outcomes. The larger the variance, the more risk to the investment. The variance measures the extent to which outcomes can differ from the mean. For this example, the variance is 15,625 (see Appendix 1 for the calculations).

Now consider a second investment where the two equally likely outcomes are $30 and $20 (with an expected value of $25). The variance is 25 (see Appendix 1).

In this relatively simple example, it is clear that the second investment (where the worst that could happen is a gain of $20) has less risk than the first investment (where the worst that can happen is a loss of $100). In this illustration, we can reach the same conclusion by observation as easily as we do by the mathematical calculation. The concept of variance is introduced here because we will be able to use it to generalize about the effect of different strategies.

In the above example, it is obvious which of the two investments is safer. But, again, consider the two investments, and assume you have to choose between them:

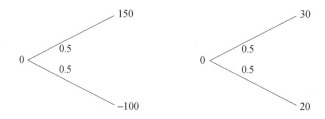

Most of us will choose the right-hand investment (a smaller variance and the same mean) but there are some decision makers who will prefer the 0.5 probability of winning $150 to a certainty of not winning an amount in excess of $30. There is not one correct decision in the choice between these two investments. The choice depends on the risk preferences of the investor, but for most of us the right-hand investment will be preferred.

Now we add a third investment that is similar to the second investment except that the two outcomes are now $40 and $20 with an expected value of $30. The variance is now 100 (see Appendix 2). Compared to the second investment, the variance has increased from 25 to 100 and the mean has increased from 25 to 30.

Inspection reveals that this third investment dominates the second investment. Equally likely outcomes of $40 and $20 are better than equally likely outcomes of $30 and $20. The larger mean for the third investment is a plus factor for the third investment. The larger variance (four times as large), however, may incorrectly scare us away from the third investment. This would be unfortunate since any investor who preferred more to less would prefer the third investment to the second. This example acts as warning against placing blind faith in the statistical measures of mean and variance, and automatically assuming that a larger variance means more risk. There is a larger spread of outcomes. The mean and variance do not capture all the information about the distribution of outcomes, thus can give incorrect signals to an investor.

Nevertheless, we will find it very useful in discussing investments to speak of means and variances of investments and portfolios. We need summary measures of the outcomes arising from investments in complex securities and these two measures have been chosen.

Managing Risk: Using Multiple Baskets

The first practical lesson of risk management is "Don't put all your eggs in one basket". Diversification is a simple, easily understood directive that is likely to be correct. Using multiple baskets has the very desirable effect of reducing the probability of the bad events. Diversification has the undesirable characteristic of reducing the probability of making very large gains.

Under what conditions is it desirable to use more than one security? The first necessary condition is that the investor has a desire to avoid risk. If the investor is indifferent to risk, then there is no incentive to use more than one security. Choose the "best" investment and bet your entire wealth on it if you are indifferent to risk. This is not an acceptable strategy for most of us.

The second necessary condition for diversification to be desirable is that alternative investments not be perfectly dependent (perfectly correlated). That is, the investments are not so linked that if one fails they all fail. With perfect dependency if one egg basket drops, all the baskets drop.

We will assume the investor is risk adverse, and the investments are independent of each other. With independence, if we know the outcome of one investment it tells us nothing about how the other investments will turn out.

Consider the investment with two equally likely outcomes of a $150 gain and a $100 loss.

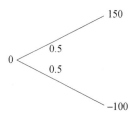

In the previous section, we computed the expected return in this situation to be $25 and the variance to be 15,625. Assume that the 0.5 probability of losing $100 is more risk than our investor wants. The investment has a positive expected value but a 0.5 probability of losing $100 is too much risk to be acceptable. How can the investor change the nature of the gamble?

Assume there is another investment with exactly the same risk characteristics, but the outcomes of this second investment are independent of the returns of the basic investment. If the investor takes one half of the two investments, the outcomes of each investment are a $75 gain and a loss of $50. The situation is now:

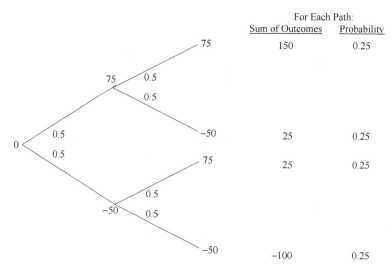

Half of the probability weights have been taken from the extreme outcomes of $150 and −$100 and shifted to the less extreme outcome of $25. The expected value is unchanged at $25. The variance, however, is now reduced to 7,812.50 (see Appendix 3).

When we invested in one project, the variance was $15,625 and by investing in two identical but independent projects the variance is now $7,812.50. Note that the new variance is half of the old variance. In fact, we can generalize. With independent identical investments and equal investments in each, the new variance is:

$$\text{New Variance} = \frac{\text{Variance of Basic Investment}}{\text{Number of Different Investments}}$$

If enough independent investments were added, the variance of the investment portfolio would approach zero.

The gains in risk reduction from diversification are dramatic. The second independent investment (the first one added to the basic investment) cuts the risk as measured by the variance in half. The mean value does not change, thus the investor who is not concerned with risk (is not risk adverse) will not bother to spread out over many different investments. The risk adverse investor has an incentive to diversify, even though the probability of the largest gain is reduced. Diversification leads to a reduction in the probability of gaining the largest outcome and a reduction in the probability of the largest loss.

In this section, we are considering only independent investments. Later in the chapter, we shall see that the assumption of independence is not necessary for achieving a large amount of diversification.

Up to this point, we have assumed that not only are the investments independent, but that they also had equal variances. If they have different sized variances and the same mean, we can still reduce the size of the portfolio's variance by investing in both investments. The optimum split will depend on the relative size of their variances. The exact solution is not important to this discussion, but it is important to recognize that with independent investments having the same expected value (or having the same expected return) all the investments will be incorporated into the final portfolio. There will be more funds invested in the small variance investments than the large variance investments, but all will be represented.

If the means of the individual investments are not equal we cannot be sure that larger variance investments with smaller mean values will enter the final solution, but they might.

If the outcomes are not independent we can still reach some general conclusions. If the alternatives all have the same mean, then some amount of each alternative should be incorporated in the final portfolio. Even though the outcomes are highly correlated (but not perfectly correlated) some risk reduction is obtained by adding the security to the collection of investments (the portfolio). If the variance of the investment being considered is relatively large, then only a small amount of that investment will be added.

The ultimate diversification tool is a negatively correlated investment. Negative correlation means that when one investment goes up, the other investment goes down.

Consider the following two investments where there are two possible events; Sunshine and Rain:

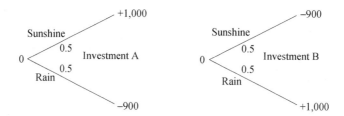

Both of the investments have positive expected values and are acceptable unless the investor is adverse to risk. However, the fear of losing $900 with 0.5 probability may scare off some investors.

If Sunshine occurs, investment A pays $1,000 but investment B loses $900. If Rain occurs, investment A loses $900, but B pays $1,000. If both investments are undertaken, we have:

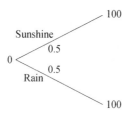

The investor receives a net payoff of $100 independent of the event that occurs. The two investments are perfectly negatively correlated. The correct mixture of investments (one of each) completely eliminates risk and insures that there will be a gain.

Negatively correlated investments (one goes up when the other goes down) are scarce in the real world, however, there are a few widespread examples. Life and fire insurance are two examples. With life insurance, if one lives, paychecks are received and the life insurance is a waste. If one dies, the paychecks stop but the life insurance pays off.

Lacking a large number of negatively correlated investments which would completely eliminate risk, the investor seeking to reduce risk turns to investments that are less than perfectly correlated. If investments were all perfectly correlated, spreading one's investment funds over the different investments would not reduce risk. With less than perfectly correlated investments, the addition of a variety of investments reduces risk.

Thus, diversification leads to a reduction of risk in all situations except where the investments are perfectly correlated (if one basket is dropped they all drop). We have assumed all investments have the same mean because in the absence of this assumption we would not be able to make the same general conclusions, but diversification would still be desirable.

Many of the investment recommendations to follow will be based on the desire to reduce risk by diversification. This is the beginning of the explanations that will help us understand how diversification can be achieved.

The Ultimate Tool of Analysis: The Covariance

This section can be omitted on a first reading of this book.

To this point we have used the variance of the outcomes of an investment as the relevant measure of risk. If we are comparing the risk of one portfolio of assets to a second portfolio we would use the variances of the two portfolios as measures of risk. This remains unchanged.

However, if we are evaluating the risk of a component part of a portfolio, the relevant measure of risk is not the "variance" but rather the "covariance" of the investment with the other parts of the portfolio. The covariance becomes the ultimate tool of analysis in forming portfolios. One cannot understand investment strategy without appreciating the importance of the covariance of an investment. The covariance measures the degree and type of relationship with the other components of the portfolio.

Consider investment A with the following outcomes:

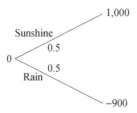

This investment has an expected value of $50 and a variance of 902,500 and since there is a 0.5 probability of a $900 loss this is a very risky investment. The calculation of the variance is:

$$(1{,}000 - 50)^2\,0.5 = 451{,}250$$
$$(-900 - 50)^2\,0.5 = \underline{451{,}250}$$
$$902{,}500$$

Now assume a second investment that is negatively correlated with the first investment. This is investment B.

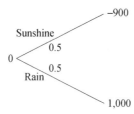

This investment also has an expected value of $50 and a variance of $902,500. However, the covariance of the two investments is large and negative (we compute it in Appendix 4). The covariance is negative 902,500. To find the variance of a portfolio of two investments, we add the variances of each investment and add two times the covariance of the two component investments:

$$\text{Variance (Portfolio)} = \text{Var(A)} + \text{Var(B)} + 2\text{Cov(A, B)}$$
$$= 902{,}500 + 902{,}500 + 2(-902{,}500) = 0.$$

In deciding whether to add investment B to the portfolio the fact that B was very risky with a large variance was not relevant. The covariance of B and A was very relevant. The negative covariance resulted in risk being completely eliminated (the investments are perfectly negatively correlated). The variance of the portfolio after adding B is equal to zero.

The above example illustrates the importance of the covariance, but not its calculation. There are several ways of defining and computing the covariance. The important characteristic to note is that if the outcomes of the two investments are highly dependent (if one goes up the other goes up) the covariance will be positive and relatively large. The risk of the portfolio is larger than if the covariances were small or negative. If the two investments are highly negatively correlated (if one goes up the other goes down) the covariance will be negative and relatively large. The risk of the portfolio will be smaller than with a large positive covariance. If the degree of association between the investments is small, the covariance will be relatively small.

We have indicated that the variance of a portfolio of two investments is equal to the sum of the variances of each of the investments plus two times the covariance. If there are three investments, we have the sum of three variances plus two times three different covariances. If there are five investments there are five different variances plus two times ten different covariances (twenty covariances).

The number of covariance for n different investments is:

$$\text{Number of Covariances} = n^2 - n$$
$$\text{With } n = 100$$
$$\text{Number of Covariances} = 9,900.$$

In computing the variance of the portfolio consisting of 100 different investments, there will be 100 variances summed plus 9,900 covariances. The covariances tend to overwhelm the variances in importance in the calculation of the portfolio variance.

Now let us apply the above specific formulations in a more general way. We will assume a set of securities all with the same variance and the same degree of association (the exact expression is that they all have the same correlation coefficient). If we invest in only one security we will assume there are 100 units of risk as measured by the variance.

If we split the investment between two securities we will achieve half of the maximum feasible risk reduction. If we invest equally in ten different securities we will achieve 9/10 of the maximum feasible risk reduction. For example, if the investments are all independent of each other then the portfolio of ten different securities would have a variance of ten compared to a variance of 100 with one security.

While further risk reduction can be achieved by adding more securities the amount of risk reduction achieved by spreading the investment over as few as ten different securities is dramatic. The feasible reduction as a percentage of the maximum reduction that can be achieved is:

$$\frac{n-1}{n},$$

where n is the number of securities.

The basic message of this book is to make use of the above relationships as a general decision tool. Diversifying in a reasonable, intelligent fashion will greatly decrease the risk facing the investor. Diversification does not increase the expected return but it does shift probability weights from the large negative outcomes to more easily digestible less dramatic outcomes.

Summary

This chapter offers calculations that can help determine the likelihood and amount of gain and the amount of risk associated with an investment. They will not insure that you will undertake the "correct" investment, but they are helpful in describing the investment that you are considering.

This chapter also introduces the important concept of unfair and fair gamble. A bet at a gambling device in Las Vegas is unfair and a purchase of a common stock is a fair gamble.

Diversification reduces the probabilities of the extreme outcomes. To reduce the probability of a large loss is good. To reduce the probability of a large gain is bad, but it is the price we have to pay to reduce risk using diversification.

If you like to gamble
And have money to spare,
Stick to stocks and to bonds
Where the gamble is fair

Florence M. Kelso

Appendix 1

Computation of the Variance

Mathematically, the variance (Var) is defined as: Var = Sum of [(Outcome − Mean)^2 × Probability of Outcome] for all outcomes. Continuing the example where the two equally likely outcomes are $150 and −$100 and the investment has a mean outcome of $25, we have for the calculation of variance:

$$(150 - 25)^2\,0.5 = \quad 7,812.50$$
$$(-100 - 25)^2\,0.5 = \quad \underline{7,812.50}$$
$$\text{Var} = \underline{\underline{15,625.00}}$$

The variance (or spread) is 15,625. The standard deviation (square root of the variance) is 125. The outcomes have a large amount of spread compared to an investment where the two equally likely outcomes are $30 and $20 (again, with an expected value of $25). The calculation of the variance for this investment is:

$$(30 - 25)^2\,0.5 = 12.50$$
$$(20 - 25)^2\,0.5 = \underline{12.50}$$
$$\text{Var} = \underline{\underline{25.00}}$$

This second investment has a variance of 25 and a standard deviation of 5 compared to a variance of 15,265 and a standard deviation of 125 with the first investment.

Appendix 2

Now consider an investment with two outcomes $40 and $20 with an expected value of $30. The variance is now:

$$(40 - 30)^2\, 0.5 = 50$$
$$(20 - 30)^2\, 0.5 = \underline{50}$$
$$\mathrm{Var} = \underline{\underline{100}}$$

Appendix 3

Assume three outcomes

Cash Flow	Probability	Expectation
150	0.25	37.5
25	0.50	12.5
−100	0.25	−25.0
	Expected Value	25.0

The calculation of the variance is:

$(\text{Outcome} - \text{Mean})^2$	Probability		Product
$(150 - 25)^2$	0.25	=	3,906.25
$(25 - 25)^2$	0.50	=	0
$(-100 - 25)^2$	0.25	=	3,906.25
	Var	=	7,812.50

Appendix 4

Calculation of Covariance for Sunshine — Rain Example

Covariance (A, B) = Average of the product of the outcomes for A and B
for all events minus the product of their means

For example, we have:

Event	Outcome of A		Outcome of B		Probability		
Sunshine	1,000	×	−900	×	0.5	=	−450,000
Rain	−900	×	1,000	×	0.5	=	−450,000

$$
\begin{array}{rr}
\text{Average of the product} & -900,000 \\
\text{Mean of A} \quad \$50 & \\
\text{Mean of B} \quad \times 50 & -2,500 \\
\hline
\text{Covariance} & -902,500 \\
\hline
\end{array}
$$

Questions

1. A gamble costing $200 has the following two outcomes:
   0.3   1,000
   0.7   0
   a. What is the expected value of this gamble?
   b. Is this a fair gamble?

2. There are ten independent investment alternatives each with a variance of outcomes of 100,000.
   Buying equal amounts of each of the ten securities, the variance of the portfolio will be _____.

3. Assume a gamble has two equally likely outcomes, 50 and 30.
   a. Compute the expected return.
   b. Compute the variance.
   c. Compute the standard deviation.

4. Compare the riskiness of the gamble of problem 3 with the riskiness of the gamble described in the chapter where the two outcomes were $30 and $20.

Chapter 4

Types of Financial Securities

In this chapter, we will consider, from the point of view of the individual investor, the return-risk characteristics of five basic types of securities issued by corporations and the financial markets:

a. Corporate bonds,
b. Preferred stock,
c. Common stock,
d. Convertibles, and
e. Other.

Corporate Bonds

A corporate bond is a debt of a corporation. If the corporation fails to make timely payments of interest and principle, the bondholders can force the corporation into bankruptcy. The bonds have payment priority over common stock and preferred stock.

A corporate bond promises to pay interest (conventionally twice a year on specified dates) and principle at maturity but some bonds make only one payment at maturity.

When the market interest rate goes up, the present value of a bond's future cash flows goes down and the market price of the bond goes down.

Corporate bonds are the safest of the financial securities issued by a corporation, but even among corporate bonds there are large differences in risk. These differences arise because firms differ in their ability to pay the contractual amounts, as well as because one corporation can issue different types of bonds with different safety features. The contractual provisions of the bonds will affect the risk of the debt security. In addition, even if the corporate bond is very high quality the purchaser has the risk that interest rates will go up and the value of the bond will go down. For example, during the inflationary period of the seventies interest rates kept going up and bond prices kept going down. This can be a shock to the investor seeking safety in the purchase of high quality corporate bonds and finding instead a decreased investment value both in real terms and in terms of dollars.

Thus even the best debts of the most financially sound corporation have risk attached to them. The amount of risk will be a function of the economic life of the debt, that is, how rapidly the cash flows will be received back (the average life is sometimes called the duration of the debt).

Despite the admission that all debt has several risks, it is still a fact that the debt of a financially sound corporation is a relatively safe investment, at least in terms of earning a well defined dollar return.

The most significant drawback of a corporate bond to an investor subject to taxation is that the interest earned on that bond is taxed as ordinary income as it is earned. If the investor is taxed at a 0.34 marginal rate (federal plus state plus city), the taxation reduces the return. With common stock, the tax rate on dividends and capital gains are both lower than 0.34 in the U.S.

A bond that was originally issued at par offers the possibility of capital gains taxation if interest rates have gone down since the bond was purchased. On the other hand, assume the interest rate has gone up. If the bond has many years to go until maturity and if the increase in interest rates has been large, the price decrease from the par (maturity) value of the bond will be large and we will have a "deep discount bond". Assume the purchase of such a discount bond. The current interest payment (which is relatively small) will be taxed as ordinary income but the increment in value each period as the bond gets closer to maturity, will only be taxed at maturity or sale and then only at the capital gains rate.

Example

Assume a bond promises to pay $1,000 at time 3 and nothing sooner. The market interest rate for this bond is 0.10. The market price is $751.315.

$$1,000(1.1)^{-3} = \$751.315$$

751.315 grows to 826.447 at time 1

826.447 grows to 909.091 at time 2

909.091 grows to 1000.00 at time 3.

Zero coupon bonds are issued by corporations (and other entities). They do not pay interest currently but rather they pay one amount at maturity. These bonds sell at a discount at time of issue. Unlike deep discount bonds that were issued at face value, the increment in value each period as the bond gets closer to maturity is taxed as ordinary income. Only if a bond decreases in value after issue is the capital gains treatment at maturity on value increases allowed.

In general, high tax rate investors do not find corporate bonds selling near par to be an attractive investment. If they want the safety of bonds, they are more likely to invest in tax exempt government securities than they are to invest in corporate debt where the interest income is taxable as ordinary income. The after tax return from a 0.10 corporate bond is 0.066 if the investor is paying taxes at the rate of 0.34. There are likely to be tax exempt debt investments that offer the possibility of a higher after tax return with either less risk or only slightly more risk.

If the investor has a tax rate close to zero, then corporate debt may become an attractive investment for the investor who wants a relatively safe cash flow stream. Corporate bonds are reasonable investments for retirement accounts that are not taxed currently (such as Keough, 401 K, or IRA's).

There are private agencies who rate the debt of corporation according to the amount of risk associated with the securities. The highest rating offered is AAA and the next highest rating is AA. These are extremely high ratings and one can accept these ratings as evidence that competent honest analysts have found these securities to be relatively immune from default risk.

The next lower rating is A and then we go to BBB (different agencies use slightly different letter designations) and that is about as low in ratings as an investor in debt wanting to avoid significant default risk should go. Below BBB the debt becomes more like a risky gamble than a safe investment. There is nothing wrong in undertaking risky investments, but the investor should be aware of the magnitude of risk.

As one slides down the ratings scale, one can increase the contractual return. Unfortunately there is no free lunch. There is more risk with a BBB bond than with a AAA bond and while there is reason to think that on the average the actual realized return with the BBB bond will be larger, there is also a larger risk of loss. Some independent studies have indicated the rating agencies make reasonably accurate estimations of risk. While there are periods of time when the average return from BBB debt have exceeded the average return from AAA debt, the evidence also shows there is more risk. As long as you are willing to accept the higher risks associated with the lower rated bonds, there is nothing wrong with seeking out the higher contractual returns.

Bond investment funds face competition for customers and investment funds will try to achieve an attractive contractual yield. One way to increase the yield of a portfolio is to accept lower rated securities into the portfolio. Before buying a bond investment fund you should be sure the ratings of the bonds in the portfolio are consistent with your investment objectives.

Corporate bonds are subject to "event risk". Event risk takes place when the corporation changes its characteristics in significant ways. The event is likely to be a surprise to the bond owners and can be a surprise to management. This might take place because of a change in strategy but it can also take place because of merger and acquisition events. The investor can buy a triple A bond but then have the corporation merged into a very risky acquiring corporation. The change in corporate structure can result in the triple A bond becoming a double B bond. Many recently issued bonds offer event risk protection.

Preferred Stock

The second type of security to be considered is preferred stock. Preferred stock is an equity security and offers little legal protection to its owners (unlike debt). While preferred stock is senior to common stock it is junior to debt. The promise to pay preferred stock dividends is normally well defined for the specific stock (say, $3 per year) but the payment is conditional on the board of directors deciding that a dividend is desirable. If a company does not pay bond interest when due, the bondholders can force bankruptcy. The penalty to a corporation of not paying a preferred stock dividend is of a smaller magnitude (the preferred stockholders may be represented on the board of directors) than with debt. Therefore the preferred stockholders have only a modest amount of protection against a corporation omitting the payment of dividends. Preferred stock is riskier than debt though safer than common stock.

Normally preferred stock yields a slightly lower return than the debt of the same firm. Both the debt interest and some preferred stock dividends are taxed as ordinary income. The preferred stock has more risk than the debt of the same firm. The individual investor can get more risk and a lower return from investing in the preferred stock than by investing in a bond issued by the same firm. For an individual, investing in preferred stock tends to be dominated by investment in debt or common stock (corporations on the other hand have tax incentives for investing in preferred stock), but it is necessary to do the calculations.

We need to explain why the preferred stock will tend to yield less than debt securities of the same risk. Corporate investors in preferred stock tend to have a 70% dividend received deduction. Only corporations have a dividend received deduction. A corporation receiving $100 interest and paying 35% tax will net $65. The same corporation receiving $100 preferred stock dividend will only be taxed on $30 of dividends and this results in $10.50 tax. The firm nets $89.50. Because of the 70% dividend received deduction, the investing corporation can accept a lower dividend with preferred stock than the $100 interest and still beat the return from the debt.

Common Stock

The third security to be considered is common stock, the residual ownership in a corporation.

An advertisement for Amax Inc. in the September 28, 1981 issue of the *Wall Street Journal* indicated that if you own one share of Amax stock you owned (reserves per share):

Molybdenum 12.5 tons of ore,
Coal 53.6 tons,
Petroleum 0.2 barrels,
Natural Gas 5,315 cubic feet,
Copper 3.7 tons of ore,
Potash 1.2 tons of ore,
Phosphates 9.1 tons of ore,
Iron Ore 7.4 long tons of ore,
Lead and Zink 01.4 tons of ore,
Tungsten 0.04 tons of ore,
Silver 0.13 tons of ore.

The advertisement dramatically pushed home the fact that when you buy a share of common stock you are buying a percentage of the ownership of that company. Amax owns coal reserves of 3.3 billion tons. Dividing by the number of outstanding shares we obtain the 53.6 tons number indicated above.

The fact that a share of common stock represents ownership in a corporation that owns valuable assets is sometimes neglected by investors. Some investors have a tendency to look at the purchase of common stock as being the equivalent as the purchase of a lottery ticket. It is true that the stock price may go up or down but behind the easily observable market price are the real assets whose value is much more difficult to determine. For example, if the coal reserves are readily available for strip mining their value is different than if they are deep in the ground and the potential coal mine has not yet been developed.

Also, the above listing of resources is incomplete because there is no indication of other claims on these assets such as liabilities or long term contracts to supply the resources at prices that are not very profitable. Nor are the costs of bringing the resources to market revealed. The partial analysis may be misleading, if not in the case of Amax, then in the case of the next company we consider.

Common stock offers the possibility of both dividends (taxed at special rates or ordinary rates) and price appreciation (taxed at capital gains rates). The short run dividends are somewhat more easily predicted than the price appreciation. The price appreciation is affected not only by how well the firm does, and interest rates, but also by the overall level of the stock market and the market's perception of the stock's value. Thus an analyst forecasting a return for a common stock is concerned with the future dividends and the future earning, as well as what is going to happen to the market. Forecasting what is going to happen to the market is not easy.

Let us assume that a stock is selling at $100 per share and we expected the dividend to be paid one year from now to be $8 and the stock price to be $112. The return expected to be earned is:

$$\text{Expected Return} = \frac{(112 - 100) + 8}{100} = \frac{20}{100} = 0.20.$$

Note that both the future dividend ($8) and the future stock price ($112) entered the calculation of the expected return. Other formulations of expected return are possible but this format captures the basic elements.

An investment in common stock results in the purchase of part of the ownership in a corporation. If there are 10,000,000 shares outstanding and you own 100 shares, you own 1/100,000 of the stock equity of the firm. If the firm is profitable and if dividends are paid and/or the stock price increases and if other investments do not earn a larger return, you might get a return that will make you happy. A lot of favorable events have to happen for an investor in common stock to earn a good return.

Frequently people look at common stock as an opportunity to gamble. It is hoped that the stock price will go up in a very short time period and large gains will be made. Day traders are an extreme example of this type of person. The stock market price is frequently disassociated in the minds of the public from the fact that the firm owns and operates assets and it is this operation of assets that is going to lead to gains or losses. The whims of buyers and sellers in the market are much less important in the long run than the underlying economic success or failure of the corporation in its business activities. This point of view assumes the intrinsic value of the security will be the most important single factor in the setting of the stock price.

Common stocks are a reasonable vehicle for investment, but a short-run gambling strategy is different from investing. The primary problem in using common stock for gambling purposes is that there are significant transaction costs associated with buying and selling common stock. If the investor engages in a great deal of churning of the portfolio, it is very difficult to earn a positive return. If it costs 0.03 to buy and 0.03 to sell, then two sets of selling and buying will tend to eat up the return earned in a normal year. The investor will claim that the selling and buying is taking place to enhance the portfolio. However, for every seller who thinks it is time to sell there is a buyer who thinks it is time to buy. All the traders in common stock cannot be right.

Common stocks are a reasonable long-term investment. They are probably no worse a short term speculation than most other short term speculations (they are as good as Las Vegas or the local race tracks), but that does not mean that short term speculation is likely to be profitable. The evidence indicates that common stock returns have been more than competitive in the long run with the returns offered by other types of investments. While the actual results will depend on the period studied, strong arguments can be offered for including common stock in any portfolio of assets being held for income purposes.

The widespread of outcomes with common stock investments means that there can be years when an investment shows a low or negative return. Thus if there is a strong probability of needing a given amount of cash on a given date, common stock is not the best investment.

We can learn from history but we should not assume that the future will be exactly the same as the past. One important lesson that we learn from history is that events that have not been predicted will occur. We can be certain that surprises will occur. Thus our financial strategy must be broad and encompass a wide range of investments. The historical returns indicate that common stock should be an important part of such an investment strategy.

If common stock earn a 0.10 return (an above average return) and if you pay a financial planner a 0.05 fee for designing your portfolio, then the planner gets 50% of your return. Of course if you earn 0.25 and everyone else earns 0.10, then the planner getting 0.05 still leaves you with 0.20, a very healthy return. But it is very difficult to earn 0.25 when the market earns 0.10 unless you use a large amount of debt leverage.

Convertibles

There are securities that do not classify neatly as either debt or stock equity since they are hybrids. While some of these securities are relatively easy to value, others are extremely complex. In fact, one of their advantages may well be that the company issuing them, and the investor receiving them, may have entirely different estimates of value (this can be useful in negotiations for acquiring firms). While both preferred stock and bonds may have conversion features, the discussion here will be made in the context of convertible debt. A convertible bond is a debt security that can be converted into common stock (usually of the corporation that issued the bond) when the owner of the bond desires to convert.

Convertible debt securities are popular among investors who want some fixed (well-defined) income but do want to have a probability of larger gains. The convertible feature opens up the possibility of large gains if the stock appreciates in value, but there is only a small probability of large losses because of the security's bond characteristics. The bond feature tends to guarantee the payment of principal at a given maturity date (if the bond is not paid prior to that date). These safety features are not without a cost to investors; convertible bonds carry a lower interest rate than comparable corporate bonds without the conversion feature.

Both bonds and preferred stock are often convertible into a common stock at a fixed ratio of shares of common stock to the senior security. This discussion of convertible securities will be in terms of convertible bonds even though the discussion also applies to convertible preferred stock.

Consider a par value $1,000 bond that is convertible into 20 shares of common stock. We would say that the conversion price is $50 per share. If the common stock goes above $50, then the conversion privilege is worth something to the investor who has to sell. The bond will sell at a value equal to or larger than its conversion value. For example, if the common stock is currently selling at $60 per share, the holder of the bond can realize at least $1,200 on the sale of the bond. Without the conversion feature an investor would only realize $1,000 if the interest rates do not change (if interest rates have fallen significantly the investor might be able to realize more than $1,000, even without the conversion feature).

A person buying a convertible bond is receiving the rights to future interest and principal payments plus the privilege to convert to common stock. The investor buys a call option on the firm's common stock with the purchase of a convertible bond. A call option gives the owner of the option the right to buy shares of a common stock from the seller of the option at a specific price (the exercise price) at any time prior to a given date (the maturity date). If at maturity of the bond the price of the common stock increases sufficiently to cause the bond price to go above the maturity value the bondholder benefits from the conversion feature. The issuing corporation benefits from the conversion feature by being able to issue debt with a lower interest rate than it would otherwise have to pay. In addition, at some time in the future it may be able to force conversion of the debt into common stock, thus decreasing the amount of debt outstanding, without making a cash outlay. Also regulated institutional investors are generally allowed to purchase convertible bonds even where they are prevented from buying call options on the common stock of the same corporation. Fringe benefits to the investor are lower margin requirements and lower transaction costs than those associated with the purchase of common stock.

An investor can borrow funds from a broker to buy securities. The broker requires the investor to put up some cash, say 20% of the amount of the investment. The 20% is the margin requirement.

Conversion terms may change through time either because of built-in conditions in the bond indenture or because of stock dividends and stock splits. The investor in convertible bonds should insist on protection clauses in the bond contract against harmful effects of stock dividends and splits.

The period of time during which the conversion features apply may not be the same as the period of time until the bond matures. It is important that the contract be read carefully by the investor so as to reduce the number of unpleasant surprises.

Investors are frequently interested in two measures: the "premium over bond value" and the "conversion premium". We will compute these measures as percentages, although they are sometimes presented in dollar amounts.

The premium over bond value is defined as:

$$\frac{\text{Market Value Now} - \text{Value of Comparable Straight Debt}}{\text{Value of Comparable Straight Debt}} \quad (1)$$

The conversion premium is defined as:

$$\frac{\text{Market Value Now} - \text{Value if Converted into Common Stock}}{\text{Value if Converted}}. \quad (2)$$

Example

An 8% $1,000 bond is convertible into 20 shares of common stock. The stock is currently selling at $45 per share and the bond is selling at $1,200. Assume the bond as straight debt would have a value of $800.

The premium over bond value is:

$$\frac{1,200 - 800}{800} = \frac{400}{800} = 0.50$$

The conversion premium is:

$$\frac{1,200 - 20(45)}{20(45)} = \frac{300}{900} = 0.33.$$

The bond is currently selling at 50% over its value as straight debt and 33% over its conversion value as common stock. Depending on the value of the implicit call option and the value of the security as debt and thus a floor, the investor should consider selling the bond.

Other factors of interest to the investor are the period during which the bond cannot be called and the call premium when it can be called. If the corporation has the option of calling an outstanding $1,000 (face value) bond for $1,050, the call premium is $50 (the call price minus the face value). The call price is defined at time of issue as part of the bond contract. The higher the call premium the more protection the investors have against being forced to sell or to convert their bonds before they want to. A called convertible bond can be converted into common stock if an investor so desires.

One criterion that corporations use in determining whether or not to call is the drain on cash resulting from the dividends on stock compared to the interest payments. If the common stock in the above example were paying $1 per share per year, conversion would mean cash dividends of

$20 per year compared to $80 per year of interest (assuming a 40% corporate tax rate, the after-tax interest cost is $48). With these alternative cash flows the corporation might well decide conversion was desirable as soon as the conversion value went above the call price (or enough above so that the investors would convert rather than take advantage of the opportunity to liquidate their investment without transaction costs). The investors for their part would compare $80 of interest and $20 of common stock dividend, the safety given by the bond feature of the security; and decide whether to postpone conversion until the cash dividend was increased or they were forced to convert by the bonds being called.

When should an investor convert? There is only one reason for voluntary conversion on the part of the investor. Investors who want to maximize the value of their cash flows should compare the interest cash flows with the debt and with the dividends on the common stock they would hold after conversion. Since they can convert at any time prior to the end of the conversion period the decision is independent of the stock price. Investors would only compare the after tax dividend resulting from holding stock and the after tax interest flow resulting from holding the bonds. They will not convert as long as the after tax annual interest flow exceeds the after tax annual dividends. If dividends now exceed interest, the investor must consider the additional return and the additional risk associated with holding stock rather than debt and receiving more risky but larger cash flows. Where the cash flows resulting from holding stock are larger than the cash flows from the debt it is not clear cut that the conversion is desirable. Giving up the safety offered by the debt form of security is a high cost that should not be incurred for marginal cash flow benefits.

One of the important advantages of a convertible bond is that it offers interesting risk possibilities. There is only a very small probability of losing large amounts and there is a high probability of large gains (if the common stock increases in value rapidly). There is also a high probability of a small loss. (This is an opportunity loss arising if the conversion feature is of little or no value ex post and only a relatively small amount of interest is earned during the life of the bond.) Since it is an opportunity loss, it is implicit rather than explicit (larger interest payments could have been earned on bonds without the conversion feature); therefore, it is not apparent to many investors. If the investor had known that the stock price would not go up, thus the bond would not be converted, the investor would not buy the convertible since the convertible will pay a smaller interest rate than a non-convertible debt issued by the same corporation.

A second advantage of convertible bonds for a speculator is that they sometimes have a smaller margin requirement than stock. Thus the investors can lever their investment with more borrowed funds invested in convertible bonds than they can invest in common stock.

Recognize that with a convertible security an investor must consider:

a. the interest or dividend being paid,
b. the conversion premium,
c. the call price,
d. the period of no-call (the call protection),
e. the expected growth rate of the common stock price.

Obviously an investor trying to place a value on a conversion feature has a major valuation problem. The conversion feature has positive value but that value may be very small depending on the values of the variables described above.

Convertible bonds may be an attractive investment in a growth situation (thus tending to ensure conversion) but where there is a possibility of the growth not taking place (thus investors are willing to pay for the downside protection). If there were no growth possibilities the investor would prefer straight debt. If there were certainty of growth (no risk of the conversion feature being worthless) the investor is likely to do better investing in the common stock or call options. Thus a convertible bond is a type of security that fills the needs for an investor with a risk preference for a large chance of a large gain and very small chance of a large loss (although there is a large chance for a small loss).

Investment Alternatives: Other

What are the alternatives to stocks and bonds? There are many good alternatives. Some are low cost and low risk. Consider the following:

1. Exchange-Traded Funds (ETFs). Less cost for investors and good diversification.
2. Variable annuities (check costs and benefits). Can be costly and the returns are likely to be uncertain.
3. Bond market index fund (municipals?).
4. Inflation-protected bonds (TIPS).
5. Mutual funds (e.g., Index Funds). Some funds cost more than others. Also, you do not control the tax effects.

6. Specific companies you know (identify the next Warren Buffett).
7. REITS (Real estate investment trusts). They distribute a large percentage of their income thus are not tax efficient.
8. A Hedge Fund. Only for the rich sophisticated investor. It is easy to choose the wrong hedge fund.
9. Private Equity. An alternative investment vehicle which should receive no more than 10% of your investment funds and where you know well the principles.

Exchange-Traded Funds (ETFs)

These funds are like mutual funds. Mutual funds are created by investment firms for individual investors (the investment firm gets fees). The investor gets diversification. The ETFs are traded on exchanges (can be bought or sold throughout the day). They are baskets of securities (e.g., S&P 500, Dow Jones, Nasdaq 100 index, bond funds, country specific, sectors) and have low annual fees (compare 1.5% of mutual fund to 0.09% S&P 500). There are tax consequences. With a conventional mutual fund, there are taxes:

1. When there are gains on sale of outstanding investments by the fund (to balance its portfolio).
2. When shareholder leaves fund (redemptions).

With a ETF: No gain if the ETF sells to meet redemption.
ETFs have been given exotic names and are well advertised.

> Spiders (SPDR): Standard & Poor's 500
> Qubes: Nasdaq 100
> Diamonds: Dow Jones Industrial Average
> VIPERS: Vanguard index participating equity receipts.

Over $161 billion has been invested in ETFs as of 2006. There are more than 150 varieties of ETFs (unit-investment trusts). The dividends of a ETF go into the investor's brokerage account. The annual fees are 0.0035 to 0.0090 (1/4 of the fees of a typical mutual fund). There is a minimum investment size. One needs to invest more than $3,000 a transaction or the investment costs are higher. The investor in an ETF gets a lot of diversification at a relatively low cost (make sure you check on the level of the fees).

ETFs have not been in existence long enough for us to be sure that they are the most efficient means of achieving diversification. While we are optimistic that they will prove to be a fine way of achieving diversification, until they are so proven, we stick with the diversification recommendation. Include some ETFs in your investment portfolio and watch their performance.

Quant Funds

Quantitative funds use computers to analyze thousands of stocks and choose those stocks for a fund that have the characteristics that a human analyst has decided are important. Among the data the computer might consider are the P/E ratio, future earnings, past growth, debt leverage, dividend policy (dividend yield and growth), share repurchase strategy (shares bought), and size of firm (and competitive position).

Obviously, the use of the computer saves the expenses of hiring a large number of analysts. But this does not mean that the expenses are low. The computer can miss a larger number of transactions than are desirable for the investors in the funds (the computer can be taught to avoid this error).

Annuity

A series of equal payments, equally spaced through time for a defined time period.

Income Annuity

A well-defined stream:

- For your life,
- For the life of you and your spouse, and
- For a limited period of time.

The investor makes an up front payment and receives a well-defined cash flow stream. The main negative aspect of an income annuity is that there is frequently a stiff set of fees, and this limits the attractiveness of income annuities.

An income annuity pays a defined amount each year for a given number of years. A popular form of annuity is to receive a single annual amount. If the buyer dies immediately after buying the annuity, the purchase price is a complete loss. To protect against this unhappy event, one can buy an annuity that offers death benefits. A husband–wife team can be a joint-life annuity where the survivor continues to receive benefits. Of course, each provision that enhances the terms of the annuity has a cost.

Variable Annuity

Amount of payment depends on performance and contract (payment for many years may be zero). The payment amounts may depend on investment performance. Again, the fees may be large. The desirability (and risk) of a variable annuity depends on the fee schedule and the types of securities selected.

Annuities come in many different forms. You can pay a lump sum to an insurance company and receive back a series of payments for a defined period of time (say 30 years) or for life or for the life of the longest lived of a husband or wife (this is an immediate annuity). Or the first payment may be delayed until a given year (this is a deferred annuity).

The amounts to be paid may be fixed by contract or may be determined by the earnings of the account.

Of course, the insurance company charges fees and will minimize its own risk.

What is the cost of a typical annuity? While the exact amounts will depend on the terms of the contract and the investment conditions at the time of the contract, a useful rule of thumb is that the cost is 100 times the monthly payment to be received. Thus if the monthly payment to be received by the owner of the contract is $1,000, the cost will be $100,000. While the above is not exact, it gives you some idea of what a buyer has to pay for an annuity.

Fund of Funds of Hedge Funds

Hedge funds are risky. The problem is that their activities and results are not immediately transparent. A hedge fund is an investment vehicle created for sophisticated and rich investors, not for an average investor. The March 9, 2006 issue of *The Wall Street Journal* reported that an Atlanta Hedge Fund had received well over $100 million to invest. Investigators found about $150,000. To earn large returns, some hedge funds engage in very risky investments.

When hedge funds first came into existence they literally hedged their investment. For example, they would buy some stocks that looked good and sell some stocks whose future did not look promising. Thus market movements could not hurt the hedged fund. More recently, hedge funds are less likely to be hedged and are more likely to be betting that some event will happen such as a merger, an acquisition, an increase in dividends, or a spin-off of assets.

To eliminate the riskiness of an investment in a hedge fund, there are now "funds of funds". A fund of funds of hedge funds buys into more than one hedge fund and the investor gets diversification by buying shares in the fund of funds. The problem is that this introduces another level of fees.

Example

Investor buys $10,000 of shares in a fund of funds. The fund of funds buy $10,000 of several hedge funds. The hedge fund has fees equal to 0.02 of the funds invested and in addition receives as fees 0.20 of the income. Assume the hedge funds earn $2,000 of income (a 0.20 return).

Hedge Fund	**Assets**	**Income**	
Fees:			
$0.02(\$10,000) = \$200$	$10,000	$2,000	0.20 Return
$0.2(2,000) = \underline{400}$		-600	
Total fees $= \underline{\$600}$		$\underline{\$1,400}$	Income After Fees

Assume that the fund of funds charges the same fees (they could be different).

Fund of Funds			
$0.02(10,000) = \$200$		$1,400	
$0.2(1,400) = \underline{280}$		-480	
Total fees $= \underline{\$480}$	Net	$\underline{\$920}$	Income After Fees

$$\frac{920}{10,000} = 0.092 \text{ Investor's return.}$$

In this example, the 0.20 return earned by the hedge fund was reduced to 0.092 for the investor. The actual fees for the hedge fund and for the fund of funds might differ (be higher or lower) but the fee magnitudes of the example are reasonable.

Inserting layers of fees makes it very difficult to earn extraordinarily high returns.

Risk

Consider a financial advisor who offers the type of advice that has a significant probability of beating the market. Consistent with previous statements, this strategy also has a significant probability of losing money.

A second financial advisor does not attempt to beat the market, but wants a nearly 100% probability of showing a net gain. The second advisor buys only short term Federal government securities. You can throw in some short term AAA industrials if you are willing to accept some default risk.

One has to consider not only the gain earned but also the opportunity cost, thus the gain that could have been earned with an alternative investment strategy.

Summary

Each type of security offers a slightly different probability distribution of outcomes (a different expected return and different risk). Thus risk preferences will greatly affect the choice of security type.

The second major factor affecting the choice of securities is the combination of the relevant provisions of the tax law and the tax situation of the investor. The investment analysis must be done on an after-tax basis. The tax considerations can greatly affect the choice of securities to go into the investor's portfolio.

Questions

1. A bond promises to pay $1,000 at time 2 and nothing sooner. The market interest rate for this bond is 0.10.
   What is the expected market price of the bond?
2. (Continue 1). What is the expected market price if the market interest rate is 0.20?
3. (Continue 1). When the market interest rate goes up the bond value changes. How?
4. A stock is selling at $40 per share. The stock price is expected to be $50 one year from today. The stock pays $2 per year dividend.
   The stock's expected return is _____.
5. (Continue 4). If the investor's time value factor is 0.12 (the investor's opportunity cost), the value of the stock to the investor is $_____.
   Should the investor buy or sell?
6. John K. has hired a financial advisor who charges 0.05 on assets managed. John K. has all his funds invested in mutual funds that incur expenses (including fees) of 0.02. The mutual fund is expected to earn 0.10. What does John K. expect to earn?

Chapter 5

Investment Tips versus an Efficient Random Walk

On January 6, many years ago, the Dow Jones Industrial Average broke 1,000. On the same day, a market forecaster sent Telex messages to subscribers of his early warning network advising them to sell all the stocks they held and to go short on stocks with the sharpest advances. On the next day, the stock market was deluged with sell orders and the Dow index dropped dramatically.

Did the forecaster correctly anticipate the drop in the market? Or did the Telexes cause the drop? Probably the market was on the edge and the forecaster pushed it over, but we do not know the answers to the above two questions.

We can expect that there will always be periods of time when the market overreacts to statements, advice, or news. If you know the market is overreacting, you can make money by going in the opposite direction. But it is very difficult to know that there is overreaction.

There are many investors who do not care what any one forecaster thinks is going to happen. They regret when an investment advisor who is not basing recommendations on theory and logic is listened to by a wide range of followers (and by non-followers who fear the followers will cause prices to change, thus they act on the advice). Many of us sit back and wait until the market settles down because we are not good at predicting how the market will react in the short-run to nonsense. If enough investors sell, even if the reasons for selling are not good, and if other investors fear that more investors will sell, the selling wave may be contagious. Unfortunately, this type of analysis goes beyond straight financial analysis into the gray area of market psychology. It is easier to analyze stocks after the fact than to forecast what will happen as events are unfolding.

In this chapter, we shift from the approximate science of investment theory to a bit of logical witchcraft, and then back to science. The chapter is partially based on analysis, but the stock market strategies and tips are based on flawed logic and forecasts that you will likely be happier if you reject than if you accept. You should demand that any tip given to you be explained so that you can evaluate and then accept or reject the recommendation.

Consider a basic relationship of stock value:

$$\text{Stock Value} = \frac{\text{Next Period's Cash Dividends}}{\text{Cost of Equity Capital} - \text{Growth Rate in Dividend}}$$

The "Cost of Equity Capital" is the annual return required by investors.

This stock price model is based on an assumption that the stock value today is equal to the present value of all future dividends and that the dividends will grow for perpetuity at a constant growth rate. These assumptions can be changed and we can obtain comparable models based on the different assumptions but this is the most common form of the model. It tends to overstate stock value since no growth rate will persist forever.

Assume that it is expected that the next year's dividends will be $10 and the investors in the common stock want a 0.10 annual return (the 0.10 return captures the effects of both dividends and capital appreciation). The dividends and stock price are expected to grow at a rate of 0.08. The model indicates the above stock has a value (price) today of $500.

$$\text{Stock Value} = \frac{10}{0.10 - 0.08} = \$500$$

If the company is earning $20 per share with a stock price of $500, the company has a price earnings multiplier of 25.

$$\text{P/E Ratio} = \frac{500}{20} = 25$$

Now assume that while the dividend is still $10 the economy enters an inflationary period with the result that interest rates increase and the cost of equity increases to 0.20 and the growth rate expectation increases to 0.10. The stock value now becomes $100:

$$\text{Stock Value} = \frac{10}{0.20 - 0.10} = \$100$$

The above stock valuation model dramatically illustrates the fact that the stock price is heavily affected by the return that the investors in the common stock require and the expected dividend growth rate. We can easily make the effect more dramatic. For example, assume that the growth rate was 0.09 when the cost of equity capital was 0.10 so that the stock value was $1,000:

$$\text{Stock Value} = \frac{10}{0.10 - 0.09} = \$1,000.$$

If the growth rate stays unchanged and the cost of equity goes to 0.20, we have the stock tumbling to $90.90:

$$\text{Stock Value} = \frac{10}{0.20 - 0.09} = \$90.90$$

You might be wondering what this has to do with a stock tip. Assume the economy has been experiencing historically high interest rates for the past ten years and the interest rate is now 0.08. Since the bond interest rate defines an opportunity cost for investors' capital there is reason to believe that the cost of equity capital for the average risk corporation is currently somewhere between 0.08 and 0.20. Let us assume a $10 dividend, a 0.15 cost of equity and a 0.05 growth rate:

$$\text{Stock Value} = \frac{10}{0.15 - 0.05} = \$100$$

and we get a stock value of $100. The distant future dividends contribute little value to the stock price because of the high time discount factor being used. Now let us assume that interest rates retreat from their historical highs so that the cost of equity capital comes down to 0.10 and the expected growth remains at 0.05. The stock value would be $200.

$$\text{Stock Value} = \frac{10}{0.10 - 0.05} = \$200.$$

The stock doubles in value as a result of the decrease in the cost of equity capital from 0.15 to 0.10.

Assume money market funds and bank certificates of deposit were yielding 0.15 to 0.20 and investors have to choose between the high short term yields and investing in common stock. The problem with using short term securities as a substitute for long term investments is that when short term interest rates drop, the yield on these securities will drop. We can expect that common stocks will increase in value with the drop in interest rates.

The optimum strategy is to stay with the short term securities until right before the drop in interest rates. The problem is that it is difficult (impossible?) for most of us (all?) to predict when the interest rate drop will take place. Investing long term funds in high yielding short term securities is a risky strategy.

Flawed Investment Strategies

There are many flawed investment strategies that too many investors find attractive. The next sections will discuss a few of them.

The Greater Fool Theory

The stock valuation model used in the previous section is based on the assumption that the stock value is equal to the present value of all future dividends. Dividends are defined here to include all cash flows from the corporation to investors. The assumption is made that the investor buys a stock for its dividends plus price appreciation but that the price appreciation only takes place because the expectation of growth of future dividends has increased or the discount rate has decreased. Dividends are defined here to include any cash flow from the corporation to its common stock investors.

There is another reason sometimes offered for the price appreciation. A "fool" bought the stock at a higher price. And why did the fool buy the stock if the dividend growth rate has not increased? Because there is a "greater fool" who will buy from the first fool. Thus a price bubble develops that is sustained by the existence of a sufficient number of fools willing to buy at ever increasing prices, even though no real value changes are taking place.

A reliance on the greater fool theory as the basis of making an investment is not recommended here. Bubbles have a tendency to burst and should be avoided.

Unfortunately, even wise people have difficulty identifying the difference between a bubble and an interesting growth situation. After the bubble has burst it is easy to second guess the investors who bought at maximum price and conclude that they were fools to buy. But if the bubble turns out to be IBM where through the years what first appeared to be a bubble turned out to be a solid value, then the purchasers move from the fool category to perceptive investors able to discern trends before the rest of us.

The greater fool theory implicitly assumes an inefficiency in the market can take place. It assumes a stock worth $100 can take on a price of $200 merely because the investors expect someone else to buy at an even higher price. An alternative interpretation is that there are differences of opinion. Assume some investors think that a $10 dividend will grow at a rate of 0.05 with a 0.15 discount rate and the stock value is $100:

$$\text{Stock Value} = \frac{10}{0.15 - 0.05} = \$100.$$

If other investors think a 0.10 growth rate will occur, the value for the stock becomes $200:

$$\text{Stock Value} = \frac{10}{0.15 - 0.10} = \$200.$$

The greater fool theory can be redefined to be a situation where investors have different expectations. We should check the value (such as expected growth) that is required to justify the market price. If we do not like the necessary assumptions to justify the stock price then we should not buy the stock.

The above stock price model assumes that growth takes place forever. A careful analyst would also use a two or three stage growth model where two or three different growth rates (or more) are assumed through time. A firm might be expected to grow at 30% for five years, then grow at 15% for another five, and then have zero growth. These types of assumptions can be incorporated into a mathematical model and a closed form solution obtained, or alternatively the calculations can be performed on a computer using the basic time value calculations. These calculations are beyond the objectives of this book.

Stop Orders

A popular device for limiting the possible loss facing an investor is to place an order to sell if the stock drops to a given price. This is called a stop order or a stop-loss order. A stop order limits the maximum loss. But it also removes the possibility of participating in a price recovery after the initial stock price decline. Stop orders are not for all investors.

For example, if the stock price is now $40 we can place an order to sell at a price of $35. Thus the maximum decrease in value suffered by the investor will be $5.

While this strategy has its supporters, one should realize that the benefits are to a large extent an illusion. Not only are you eliminating the possibility of losing more than $5 but you are also eliminating the possibility of recovering the loss if the stock bounces back from the $35 price.

Also, sometimes the order to sell at $35 cannot be exercised by the broker. The sale takes place at a lower price.

If setting the stop order at $35 (the maximum loss is $5) is good, would it not be even more desirable to set the sell price at $39? With this strategy the maximum loss is only $1. If the sell price is set at $40, then there is a maximum loss of zero, but the expectation of transaction costs is large and the likelihood of a gain is low.

If there were no taxes and no transaction costs the stop order strategy would be harmless since when the stock reaches $35 we do not know whether it will go down further or go back up, selling the stock is not an unreasonable action if the investor does not object to being invested in short-term securities. Only if we consider transaction costs do we conclude that the strategy is harmful. If we bought the stock at $40 and we consider it to be a good buy, there is no reason to sell just because the stock price goes to $35. There may be news (new information) that justifies selling, but that is separable from the stop-loss issue.

Assuming it is desirable to sell if the stock goes down, is it desirable to buy if the stock goes above $45? Some investment strategies recommend buy if the stock goes up. But it is difficult to see why buy becomes desirable just because a stock (or the market) has gone up. Where is it going next?

One valid reason for a stop order would be a type of risk aversion. If the stock price falls one may have to shift out of common stock into other securities in order to maintain the correct asset portfolio relative to expected return risk trade-offs for the new wealth position. One can understand this reason for shifting out of common stock, but as a basic investment strategy a stop order offers little advantage. Interestingly, if the investor were perfectly diversified in stocks (you held the same proportion of your portfolio in each stock as the stock value was to total value of all stocks) then if the stock went down in value more than the market no decrease in holdings would be required. In fact, more of the stock would have to be acquired. If the percentage of the portfolio invested in the security had decreased so that too small an amount was invested in the stock, to maintain the proportion invested in that security more of the security would have to be purchased.

Example

Assume initially a stock is 2% of the total stock portfolio and in dollar amounts the relationship is:

$$\frac{\text{Invested in the Stock}}{\text{Invested in all Stock}} = \frac{200}{10,000} = 0.02 \text{ or } 2\%.$$

Now assume all stocks go down by 50% and the specific stock goes down by 90%.

$$\text{New Percentage} = \frac{20}{5,000} = 0.004 \text{ or } 0.4\%$$

To maintain the 2% proportion an additional $80 of the stock must be purchased (assuming the investor adjusts the other securities in the portfolio).

Buying a Put Option

Instead of placing a stop order an investor may buy a put option. A put option gives the holder of the option the right to sell shares of a stock at a given price to the seller of the put any time up until a specified expiration date.

If a stock is selling at $40 and a stop order is placed at $35 and stock goes down to $34, the stock is sold, when it reaches $35. The investor does not participate when the stock goes back up to above $35.

If the holder of the stock purchases a put option with an exercise price of $35 the stock can be sold at any time at a price of $35. When the stock goes down to $34 the investor with the put can hold (not sell) and wait until the expiration date. If the stock bounces back up to $37 before the put expires the holder of the put to sell at $35 does not exercise the put. This is a better position than the investor who placed a stop order and was sold out at $35.

Buying a put option makes sense for an investor who will be drastically hurt if the stock price goes below the strike price (exercise price) but the investor can afford to lose the cost of the put. In addition, the investor is basically optimistic about the future of the stock and even if it goes down would like to continue to own the stock long enough to see if it will go back up.

Who writes (sells) a put? The seller of the put must buy the security at the strike price. One put writer is the gambler who believes the stock will not fall below the strike price. Thus, if Jones writes a put with a strike price of $35, and the stock never falls below $35, Jones collects the price of the put (the option premium) and makes a profit.

If the stock falls to $30 Jones must buy the stock at $35 from the buyer of the put which is better than having bought it at $40 but not as good as buying it at $30. The seller of a put, who does not have a balancing position, can lose a large amount of money with a very small (or zero) investment.

The option writer must deposit collateral with the broker to cover the possibility that the share may have to be purchased. This is the equivalent of an investment. When a market crashes (as in October 1987), sellers of puts lose their investments and much more.

Buying and Selling Options

Several years ago investors found a "sure way" to increase their returns. They sold calls (or options) on the common stock they held. Say the price of a stock is $40 and the owner of the stock sells for $2 a 60-day call on the stock at an exercise price of $45 (the owner of the option can buy at a price of $45). If the stock price does not go above $45 the seller of the call earns $2. If this is done six times during the year the investor earns $12. Without considering dividends or capital appreciation the investor earns $12 on a $40 investment or a 0.30 return.

What can go wrong with this deal from the point of view of the seller of the call? If the stock price goes up $75, the holder of the call pays the exercise price of $45. The holder of the stock (the seller of the call) receives $47 (the $2 price of the option and the $45 exercise price) for a stock worth $75. The selling of the call was (ex post) a bad decision.

Now let us consider the transaction from the point of view of the buyer of the call option. If the stock does not reach $47 the buyer loses. The maximum the buyer of the option can lose is $2. If the stock price reaches $75 the buyer wins $28 (that is $75 - 47$) for an investment of $2.

An important motivation for buying options is the leverage possibilities. Assume the buyer has $200 thus can either buy 100 options costing $2 each or 5 shares costing $40 each. With 100 options, if the stock goes up to $75 the gain is 100 times $28 or $2,800. With 5 shares the gain is $5(74 - 40) = \$170$. Obviously if you "know" the stock price will go up the options are a good buy. But we do not know the price will go up. If the price does not exceed $45 within 60 days the buyer of the options loses $200. Buying options can be exciting.

Converting a Stock into a Bond

Assume the investor in a stock wants to protect against a loss of value and buys puts with an exercise price equal to the stock's current market price. But the puts are costly so the investor sells calls and uses the proceeds to finance the puts (the calls and puts must have the same exercise price and maturity date). This is a "costless collar". Unfortunately, if the amounts are correct, the investment in stock is converted into an investment in a debt (the upside has been sold and the downside is eliminated by the purchase of the puts).

Dollar Averaging

Dollar averaging is a procedure that is periodically discovered. The technique is simple enough to execute. You invest a series of fixed sums in one common stock through time. For example, you invest $4,000 when the stock is selling at $40 and you buy 100 shares. The stock goes up to $80 and you again invest $4,000 but this time you only buy 50 shares. When the stock goes down to $20 you again invest $4,000 and you buy 200 shares. The apparent advantage of dollar averaging is that you buy more shares when the price is low than when the price is high. There is no question that the mechanics of the procedure accomplish this.

Let us consider the above example where the initial price was $40 and then the price went to $80. At the price of $80 50 shares are purchased. This is neither good nor bad. We assume $80 is the correct market price. The future price may be higher or lower but we expect to earn a normal return on the investment.

We did not know that after increasing to $80 the stock will then drop to $20. If we knew that the price was going to drop to $20 reasonably soon, we would not have bought at $80. With a price of $80, the future is uncertain and the stock is at least as likely to go up as it is to go down.

If the stocks were to fall to $20 we cannot say that buying 200 shares, and keeping the incremental investment at $4,000 each transaction, is good or bad. Again, the $20 is likely to be a fair price and that is all we can conclude.

There is one negative aspect to dollar averaging. It is a risk intensifying strategy since we repeatedly purchase shares in the same company. To avoid this tendency many investors will only make further investments if the stock goes down. The logic is that with an initial investment of 100 shares at $40, if 200 shares are purchased at $20 then the price only has to go back up to $26.67 for the investor to break even:

$$8,000 = 300p$$
$$p = \$26.67.$$

But this number of shares necessary to break-even could be decreased even further to $24 by buying 400 shares at $20:

$$12,000 = 500p$$
$$p = \$24.$$

Thus the dollar averaging strategy can seem to be improved by having the amount of the second investment larger than the first if the stock price has gone down. But since the $20 is only the fair price of the stock and not in any sense a known minimum value, a better strategy for a risk averting investor would be to diversify.

Given the nature of dollar averaging and the way people evaluate performance (in an approximate manner), it is likely that a large number of investors using it will testify to its virtues. This vote of confidence does not prove its virtues.

There may be an advantage to dollar averaging. It forces the investor to do some buying when there is pessimism in the market, as well as when there is optimism. The rejoinder to this advantage is that if the pessimism is justified, there is no special advantage to buying.

In conclusion, dollar averaging has the disadvantage of reducing potential diversification and offers no real advantages. On the other hand, it offers no significant disadvantage.

Use of Leverage

Consider the buying of convertible bonds on margin where the brokerage firm supplies the margin (or debt money). With an investment equal to 25% of the cost ($250 on a total cost of $1,000), assume the price appreciates to $1,170 in three months. This is a return of 68% on the $250 investment (interest and brokerage fees should be subtracted). The $170 divided by $250 equals 68%.

Actually the 68% understates the return earned. A profit of $117 on an investment of $250 is a return of 68% for three months, but is an annual equivalent return of approximately $68\% \times 4 = 272\%$. Consider the buying of a share of common stock at $100 and having it increase within one day to $102. That is a 2% return for the day but a $2 \times 365 = 730\%$ annual return. We can look at the results of investing in any security for a short period of time, and if we can pick the moment of time being studied, we can obtain a wide range of results.

It is true that buying a bond on margin can be a very wise action if the bond price increases. But the same leverage (margin) that is desirable if the bond price increases can cause disaster if the bond price decreases. An increase in interest rates or a decrease in common stock price expectations can both cause a severe decrease in a convertible bond price.

A margin purchase of a security is essentially the purchase of a security with borrowed funds. The borrower pays interest on the loan. Hopefully the purchase of the security will lead to a larger return than the cost of the loan. But, there is no guarantee that this will be the situation. The use of borrowed funds to purchase securities increases the risk facing the investor. It may or may not increase the actual return of the portfolio.

An Investment Strategy

A bank invested 2% of its equity investment funds in each of 50 different industries. The funds were invested in one company in each of the 50 industries. This is consistent with the diversification strategy being suggested in this book.

However, when a stock went up or down by 20% the fund sold or bought enough shares so that the stock was again 2% of the total investment. Also, stocks were eliminated if their measures of performance (e.g., return on investment) were not the best in the industry.

Having an exact 2% of the money invested in each stock (industry) does not have a theoretical foundation. Neither does adjusting the portfolio when there is a 20% change in the value of a stock.

There is no increase in expected value but there are transaction costs if transactions take place just because a stock has gone down or has gone up. Adjustments in the portfolio can take place when new funds enter the fund or are withdrawn from the fund.

If an investment of 2% of the fund in one company is 50% of the stock ownership and if 2% of the fund in a second company is 1% of the stock ownership then the fund's performance is not going to be highly correlated with the average performance of the market. Since matching the market is not the objective, why keep the 2% split exactly if it costs money to keep it?

Also, why make the adjustment to the portfolio when a 20% change takes place? This tends to insure a relative flight from firms (and industries) doing well to firms (and industries) doing less well.

Finally, if all investors buy the stock of the best company, it might well be that the common stock of the second or third best companies are better investments.

We can expect funds to arrive at simple rules since the rules are bound to appeal to someone. Also, for a short period of time if we manage enough funds each using a different set of rules we will have some winners.

The crucial question must always be, what is the theory or logic behind the rules being used? Do we accept the theory as being logical? Some would also want empirical evidence backing up the theory. Here we have to be careful since the evidence of past performance must be carefully evaluated. For example, the fact that a fund following a given set of rules beat the Standard & Poor's index of 500 stocks for a given period of time is not proof that the set of rules is superior to investing in the average of the S&P stocks.

Easy rules for beating the market do not exist. Good careful analysis of firms and industries is as close as we can come to a good system for doing better than the market.

A Contrary Investing Strategy

There are some investors who think that when the market is selling and prices are falling, they should buy. When the market is buying and stock prices are rising they should sell. This theory is based on an assumption that the market overreacts to news. If a news story breaks that should cause the market (or a specific stock price) to fall 10%, it will fall more than 10%.

Stories can be told where this happened. When Con Ed stopped paying a dividend in its common stock in the early 1970s, the stock price fell over 20 points to a price of $6. Some investors thought this was an overreaction and bought the stock. They were right.

But this one success story for the theory does not prove that the theory is always correct. With the announcement of a bad event for a firm, conservative investors will sell the firm's stock because now the security is a risky investment. Other investors sell to realize the tax loss. Still other investors with large holdings would like to sell but cannot because they fear they would further depress the market price. This is where the contrary investor serves a very useful function. The contrary investors enable the large institutional investor to unload the doggy stock. Obviously, there are dangers in being a contrary investor. The strategy should only be used where you have logical reasons for thinking there really has been an overreaction to good or bad news.

Tips

Now a tip. If you think the interest rates will be coming down drastically sometime soon, then you should be buying common stock.

It can also be argued that long term bonds and preferred stock will also benefit from a decrease in interest rates. That is true but does not knock out the recommendation to buy common stock. Common stock with a large growth factor is likely to be more sensitive to interest rate changes than either bonds or preferred stock (the technical reason is that it has a larger duration or average life). Also, bonds tend to be callable at the whim of the corporation so the upside potential is limited. Some preferred stock will also have a call provision. In addition we argue strongly that preferred stock yielding less than comparable risk debt is an inferior investment for individuals.

Is the advice to buy common stock because interest rates will fall without risk? Unfortunately, the tip has some weak points.

First, interest rates may stay high or go higher. With no decrease in interest rates it is very difficult for stock prices to rise dramatically.

Secondly, interest rates may decrease but the decrease may be accompanied by a recession with the result that the expected growth rate decreases by an equal amount and there is again no increase in stock prices (there can be a decrease in prices if dividends are then expected to grow at a much lower rate or to decrease).

Any tip is fragile. Buying stock because interest rates will decrease is based on an assumption that interest rates will decrease but business activity will stay high. Not only do you need the tip, but you also need to understand the logic on which the tip is based so that you can intelligently accept or reject the tip.

In the situation being discussed, the tip is based on a mathematical stock price model and subjective forecasts as to future interest rates. While the model is imperfect it is probably adequate as the basis of a decision such as is being considered. The weak links are the forecasts of the interest rate and the growth rate in dividends.

Not only does the forecast of the decrease in the interest rate have to be reasonably correct, but the market has to be currently using a less good forecast. If the market's forecast is exactly the same as our forecast, then the current prices of the common stock already reflect the forecasted interest rates. Even if the decrease in interest rates takes place as scheduled, abnormal profits will not occur because the common stock prices already incorporate this information. Thus to make abnormally high returns not only do we have to forecast interest rates correctly, but the forecast had to be better than the market's forecast.

It is difficult (impossible?) to use tips involving forecasts of overall market movements to make abnormal returns.

Another argument that can be used to justify investment in common stock is that the replacement cost of the assets owned by the corporations is much higher than the market price of the assets. The assumption is that the market price of the stocks must increase to a level equal to or higher than the replacement cost of the assets in order for real investment to take place. This logic breaks down in a situation when there has been rapid technological or economic change and the economic value of the asset currently owned by the firm is much lower than the replacement cost. The replacement cost as conventionally computed leaves out economic value considerations.

Despite the above reservation about equating replacement cost and value, the fact is that assets of corporations are recorded at depreciated original cost and during a period of rapid inflation this basis of accounting is likely to understate the current value of the assets. There is evidence that the current level of common stock market prices do not always immediately reflect these increases in real value.

Another problem with tips printed in books is the time lag between when the advice is offered and when the advice is read. Obviously additional information will tend to modify one's expectation (even an expert's). It would be surprising if one's forecast of the economy were not affected by elections, international tensions, the current inflation rate, etc.

A good forecaster will give ten forecasts at a given moment in time in a form that you are not likely to retain, and then remind you a year later of the two forecasts that were correct. Unfortunately, when one writes a book the forecast is read at the same time the actual results are occurring. Forecasts in book form are dangerous for one's reputation unless the forecast is general enough to survive no matter what happens, or the forecast is for the distant future.

Let us shift to investment advice of specific common stocks. First assume that you are in a high tax bracket and a specific tax provision has been passed. Consider a tax revision that led to buying public utility common stock where the company had a dividend reinvestment plan. The advantage of the public utility stock was that the dividends reinvested were not taxed currently. The maximum amount of tax free dividends was $750 of dividends for a single return and $1,500 for a joint return. The tax deferral and possible tax avoidance was a nice provision from the point of view of a high tax investor. Tax laws affect investment decisions. Unfortunately for the clever investors, this tax provision was repealed.

A second type of tip involves the recognition of a desirable corporate strategy. Again we assume a high tax investor. Assume a company which consistently buys back its common stock and has $1,000 to distribute to investors who are taxed at a 0.15 tax rate. If dividends are paid, the investors will net $850 after tax. If a corporation's own stock is acquired, each individual investor has a choice of going for increased ownership or going for the cash. Assume some investors sell, and with a $1,000 tax basis receive the $1,000 after tax. If the tax basis were zero, the investors would net $850 with a 0.15 capital gains tax. Thus the investors in the firm acquiring its own shares net between $850 and $1,000 assuming the tax basis is between zero and $1,000. The investors not wanting cash have increased ownership and pay no tax. With a cash dividend and a 0.15 tax rate on ordinary income, the investors net $850. All investors, whether or not they want cash, receive the cash dividend. The investor not wanting cash is likely to be better off with share repurchase by the corporation.

A Trip to Las Vegas

The author went to an academic conference of finance professors in Las Vegas. He checked into the conference hotel and the bell hop carried his bags up to his room. As the bell hop went to leave the room he said, "How about a tip?" The author reached into his pocket but the bell hop said, "Naw. What I want is a stock tip." The professor obliged. Unfortunately, the professor does not remember the nature of the tip. Hopefully, it was "diversify".

A Get Rich Strategy

The tips of this chapter are not very exciting bits of advice for the investor who is waiting for the tip that is going to be the equivalent of picking the winner in the Irish Sweepstakes. Sorry, but advice for becoming rich is not the nature of this book. However, let us make clear what your strategy should be (if you insist on becoming very rich or very poor). Choose the most exciting stock you can find (the stock with the most upside potential) and invest your entire savings on this stock. To leverage your investment, you should also borrow (buy on margin) or better yet, borrow funds and buy call options (to buy the stock). Now hope the stock goes up.

Is the above a desirable strategy? Most of us would reject the strategy as having too much risk. The strategies recommended in this book are less likely to lead to large riches and are also less likely to lead to a total loss of one's wealth.

An Efficient Random Walk

A capital market is a bringing together of many different buyers and sellers of financial securities. At any moment the price of any security in that market is the result of the collective judgments and more importantly, the actions, of all the buyers and sellers, as well as the non-buyer and non-sellers. The collection of all investors make up Wall Street.

Since the mid-1960s there has been increasing support for two important hypotheses. One is that stocks follow a random walk and the other is that the capital markets are efficient.

The random walk hypothesis is the older of the two theories extending back to the nineteenth century. It does not mean that a stock might not have an upward trend or a downward trend resulting from real decision being made in the firm. Random walk does mean that at a given moment in time the amount and direction of the next price change cannot be determined by looking at past price changes. The price at a given moment reflects all the information about the security that is available (this statement also applies to an efficient market). If the random walk hypothesis is correct then anyone looking at a chart of past prices is looking at historical evidence that cannot be used to predict the next price changes. There is much empirical evidence, generally accepted in the academic community, that stocks to a large extent follow a random walk.

A capital market is efficient if the prices of the securities traded promptly reflect available information. Several distinctions have been made for different degrees of efficiency.

The weak form of the efficient market hypothesis states that one cannot look at past prices to predict future price changes. It is consistent with the random walk hypothesis. The fact that a stock is at its historical high (or low) cannot be used to justify a buy or sell action. If the stock is at its historical high it may still go up tomorrow. In like manner a stock at a new low can still go lower. The weak form is more likely to be correct than not.

The semi-strong form of the efficient market hypothesis states that the market price of a security promptly reflects all publicly available information. If the market price reflects available information rapidly then for the price to change in a predictable manner would require that new information be received by the investor before the market receives it. The semi-strong form requires that many analysts be at work so that the price at all times reflects all publicly available information. Following the semi-strong form of the efficient market hypothesis one cannot consistently earn abnormal returns using publicly available information. There is considerable support in the academic community for the semi-strong form. While the market might not absorb information instantaneously, it does not take a long time.

The strong form of the efficient market hypothesis states that the market price reflects all information, whether it is public information or not. Under the strong form one could not consistently earn abnormal profits using insider information. The strong form of the efficient market hypothesis has not been proven. There is a suspicion that the use of good insider information, while it might be illegal and unethical, is likely to lead to abnormal profits.

The implications of the above theories are important. Assume one believes that random walk and the weak form of the efficient market hypothesis, the investor does not buy or sell because of publicly available information unless he/she has reason to believe he/she is one of the early recipients of the information. Remember, the information rapidly influences the stock price.

Does the efficient market hypothesis mean that all the money spent analyzing stocks and other securities is a waste? Not at all. If there were not a great deal of analysis the market would not be efficient (or at least would be less efficient).

Does the efficient market hypothesis mean that marginal investors can assume that others are doing the necessary analysis, thus they can accept the stock prices as being efficient, and avoid the cost of additional analysis? That is an implication.

There will always be stories "proving" the market is not efficient. The rejoinder is that these anecdotes are not proof that the market is not efficient. Proving that the market is efficient or inefficient requires an accepted perfect model of the market which can then be tested. Such a model does not currently exist. Approximations do exist.

Several years ago the author ate in a Texas cafeteria, liked the meal and bought the parent company's common stock. The stock was then sold at an abnormal profit. Was the market not efficient or was this the example of a large gain to balance out the large losses that have occurred with other investors buying the stock of other food service chains and losing? The semi-strong efficient market hypothesis is not going to be knocked out by a few success stories. There is evidence that stock prices do rapidly reflect publicly available information (in some cases where leaks are feasible the information is systematically anticipated).

The investment strategy implications are clear if one accepts as reasonable approximations the random walk or the efficient market hypothesis. The amount of trading is drastically reduced since there is less confidence that one can beat the market by applying a simple filter rule (such as sell when the stock reaches a low or high price) or by applying logic using available public information. The fact that some investors do beat the market in some years can be said merely to reflect the fact that there are a large number of investors trying to beat the market, and some will succeed.

A person rejecting the random walk or the semi-strong form of the efficient market may claim there can also be success in investing based on careful intelligent analysis done in a better manner than by other analysts. While analysis is likely to have value at the margin, one has to be careful that the analysis does not lead to account churning with resulting higher transaction costs.

The Beta Factor (The Capital Asset Pricing Model)

In the mid-1960s the capital asset pricing model (CAPM) was born. Its impact on the investment strategy applied to capital market securities has been dramatic.

Theoretically one can compute the mean and variance of all possible sets (combinations) of securities. From all the portfolios we will choose the best portfolios and construct an "efficient frontier". What do we mean by "best portfolio"? For each expected return, the portfolio having the smallest variance is best. Equivalently, for each variance the portfolio having the largest mean return is best.

If we combine the best of the set of efficient portfolios (this portfolio is called the market portfolio) with default free government securities (the amount of government securities may be zero if the investor has strong risk preferences) with the risk preferences of the investor we obtain the optimum portfolio. The amount of government securities will depend on the risk preference of the investor but all investors who buy stocks will hold the market portfolio because that set of securities dominates all others. If a security is not in the market basket of securities its price will fall until it is attractive enough to enter the market portfolio.

All risk associated with a security is divided into two parts; the systematic risk and the unsystematic (or residual) risk. The systematic risk is the risk that arises because the security's return will change as the market's return changes. The unsystematic risk arises from all other causes but is independent of the level of the market's return. If an investor holds the market basket of securities the investor is perfectly diversified, and the unsystematic risk for this investor is equal to zero and does not affect the return required by the investor. On the other hand, the systematic risk of a security very much affects the return required by investors. The measure of systematic risk conventionally used is the Beta of a security.

The Beta of a security measures the percentage change in return that can be expected for a given percentage change in the market's return. For example, if the market return increases by 0.10, a stock with a Beta of one will also have an increase in its return of 0.10.

If a security has a Beta larger than one it will be more volatile than the market. If it has a Beta less than one it will be less volatile than the market. When an investor expects the market to increase in value, it is desirable to hold a high Beta portfolio. The opposite is true if one expects the market return to decrease. If one is not willing to forecast the market return, then it is reasonable to aim at a Beta of one by investing in the market basket of securities. If the market goes up, one is then happier than with a low Beta portfolio. If the market goes down then one is less sad than with a high Beta portfolio.

Assume we want to determine whether or not a manager of a portfolio did a good job, and that we find the portfolio earned a higher return than earned by the market. Does the manager deserve praise? We should determine the Betas of the portfolio. If the portfolio had a Beta larger than one there is more risk than the market and the higher return might just compensate for the larger risk rather than showing that there was superior investment management.

The Beta is related to the required return of a security in an exact manner. The basic relationship for the required expected return for a security is:

Expected Return = Risk Free Return

$$+ \text{(Market's Expected Return} - \text{Risk Free Return)}\beta$$

where the β is the Beta of the security. For example, if a stock has a Beta of 1.2, the market has an expected return of 0.16 and the risk free return is 0.10, the security needs an expected return of 0.172.

$$\text{Required Expected Return} = 0.10 + (0.16 - 0.10)1.2 = 0.172$$

If the current price of the security lead to an expected return of 0.20, we can expect the price of the security to increase until the expected return falls to 0.172.

Not all investors are perfectly diversified, thus the model does not apply exactly to these investors. Some investors not perfectly diversified will want to consider the unsystematic risk as well as the systematic risk in determining the required expected return of a security. The Beta measure of a stock captures a large amount of useful information, but also a great deal of information is omitted. Not all investors will want to base an estimate of risk solely on the Beta measure. For one thing, the Beta of a company's common stock is not likely to be stable. It is likely to change depending on the time period over which it is measured, even where the activities of the firm are not changing perceptively. Secondly, a stock may have a Beta of one (a conservative stock) but the company may be on the verge of bankruptcy (there is unsystematic risk).

The Beta of a portfolio tells us something of its relative volatility, where the volatility is caused by market changes. As such, it is a useful measure. It is a less useful device for "beating" the market and earning abnormal returns unless your equivalents of the Betas for the securities being analyzed are better than the Betas (or other methods of analysis) that the rest of the market is using.

Summary

We are now ready for some simplified conclusions. They are:

1. Diversify.
2. Taxes (institutional factors) are relevant.
3. Markets are relatively efficient.

4. Basic analysis is useful.
5. Do not rely on someone dumber than you to bale you out.
6. Beware "rules of thumb" without theory.
7. Market turns are difficult to predict.
8. There are risk and return trade-offs.
9. The stock market throughout history has been a "fair gamble" and you should always own some stock. The casino in Ledyard, Connecticut offers "unfair" gambles.

Investing sensibly in the stock market is frustrating. If the stock you buy goes down, you know you made a mistake. If the stock you buy is a winner, the likelihood is that you are going to be sad that you did not buy more shares. Following this thinking to its logical conclusion, one cannot invest in the stock market and expect to find happiness as a result of the investment outcomes, unless you adopt a relatively passive investment strategy. You must realize that you are unlikely to beat the market. You must not rely on tips and instead you should widely diversify. Some investments will lose and some will win and you will be philosophical with both.

There is an often quoted *Wall Street* wisdom and I never understood the point of the wisdom until recently. The wisdom goes:

"A Bull makes money
A Bear makes money
A Hog never makes anything!"

Reading Fred Schwed's classic, *Where Are the Customers' Yachts?*, I found the answer (page 6). Brokerage houses tell the above story to customers to generate business when stocks go up. A hog may make money, save transaction costs, and save taxes. Is it OK to be a hog? Yes, if it means you do not automatically sell a winner. No, if it means you borrow money to buy call options and if you win, you repeat the process.

Questions

1. A stock is paying a $5 annual dividend. Investors want a 0.15 annual return from this stock. The dividend is expected to grow at 0.10 per year. What is the stock value today?

2. (Continue 1). What is the stock value if the expected annual growth rate is 0.14?

3. (Continue 1). What is the stock value if the expected annual growth rate is 0.05?

4. (Continue 1–3). What are the P/E ratios if the firm has annual earnings of $20 per share?

5. The owner of a stock sells a call option on the stock for $4. The exercise price is $30. When the call option expires, the stock is selling for $50. How much did the seller of the call option win?

6. A stock has a Beta of one. The risk free (default free) rate is 0.05 and the market's expected return is 0.09.
   What is the stock's required expected return?

7. An investor sells a put option on a stock for $4. The exercise price is $40. When the put option expires, the stock is selling at $5.
   How much did the seller of the put win?

Chapter 6

Analysis for Buying a Stock

This chapter is relevant if you intend to invest in individual stocks. Analysis of the financial affairs of corporations you are considering investing in is highly desirable.

For most investors, there is a more useful investment strategy. I suggest you invest the portion of your portfolio that is common stock in mutual funds (especially index funds) or exchange traded funds. Check the expense ratios of the funds and the implications for taxes of the strategies and choose a respected set of funds for your investment.

Following this strategy, you will obtain nearly instantaneous and inexpensive diversification. In addition, you can bypass reading this chapter until such time that you decide to ignore the above advice.

Remember that you want your common stock portfolio to be diversified. In addition, you want other types of investment securities, beyond stocks, to be in your portfolio.

Financial Analysis

You can make common stock investment decisions involving a firm without analyzing the financial reports of the firm if you are willing to assume that other investors have been setting the market price after careful analysis. If you are not willing to make this assumption then a knowledge and analysis of the content of the financial reports is essential.

Financial statements are used for many different purposes and each different use requires somewhat different information. A bank officer approving a three-month loan is interested in different information than an investor considering the purchase or sale of common stock. An economist measuring the contribution of the firm to society would require a third set of analyses.

The financial analysis of this chapter will be aimed more at the long term investor in common stock than the short term investor. However, some consideration will be paid to the firm's ability to survive in the short run.

It should be recognized that financial analysis is an inexact art that at best leads to reasoned judgments. Financial reports present some indicators of current financial position and the direction from which the firm has come. However, we would all like the answer to the question, "what is going to happen in the future?", and unfortunately, this answer is not provided by the conventional financial statements (even if there were an attempt to provide it, it would be uncertain information). After a firm goes bankrupt there is no shortage of experts who are then able to "predict" the event. Five years or even one year before the bankruptcy, however, it may be extremely difficult to predict the fact that the firm is going to have financial difficulties. The investment banking firm of Drexel-Burnham went bankrupt when the banks decided not to extend further short term credit. Chrysler Corporation did not go bankrupt because the U.S. Government decided to guarantee the debt it needed.

There are very few firms that operate with large amounts of liquid assets readily convertible into cash (in fact, in many economies it is normal practice to operate with negative cash amounts; that is, the average firm rather than having cash has negative balances with its banks). Thus any change for the worse in a firm's economic affairs could rapidly become extremely unsettling. To a large extent firms rely on arrangements made in advance with banks (lines of credit or credit agreements) to supply resources in such situations, but even such arrangements cannot be expected to save a firm in major financial difficulty.

A firm can be presenting reasonably good statements of financial position, but if there are basic changes in the firm's competitive position taking place, disaster may be looming and the financial statements reporting the past will give little or no indication of the storm clouds. A change of crucial importance to the firm may be taking place in another company or in another country (a new product may have been developed that makes the product of the firm being analyzed obsolete or non-competitive). Or the change may be a legislative change (such as the requirement of installing more pollution control devices). Such a change may make it impossible for a specific firm to operate profitably in the future; in fact, it might well cause immediate bankruptcy, but it may not be in the financial report.

The primary point being made is that accounting information is backward looking rather than incorporating guesses about the future. Because of this characteristic, even the best accounting information must be adjusted by an investor in common stock to take into consideration future events that might occur or the future effects of events that have already taken place.

Despite the above disclaimers about usefulness, given the absence of crystal balls, there are many accounting measures that are useful to a person making an investment decision. An investor knows something of value if the earnings of a firm are $2.50 per share and they are increasing compared to another similar firm where the earnings are $0.80 per share and they are decreasing. Also, any purchaser of common stock should want to know the amount of debt that is outstanding and its characteristics, as well as the coverage ratios (such as earnings divided by interest) to gain an impression of the margin of safety (or risk) that is present.

The accountant uses explicit rules in deciding how to record financial transactions, but there is discretion in how the rules are interpreted. Thus we may find several firms recording the same financial transaction in a much different manner. This chapter will review three types of reports presented by the accountant, suggesting their uses and limitations. In addition, the types of rules that are applied by the accountant will be discussed. If the appropriate rules are followed, then the certified public accountant auditing the firm issuing the report will indicate that the financial report "was prepared in accordance with generally accepted accounting principles". The three reports we shall discuss in this chapter are the balance sheet, the income statement, and the statement of changes in financial position.

The Balance Sheet

The balance sheet of a corporation is a financial picture of the firm at a specific moment of time prepared consistent with accounting conventions. A popular form of presentation is to have the assets on one side of a page faced by the sources of assets (the liabilities and the stockholder's equity). Since the sum of the balances of each asset account is equal to the sum of the asset sources, a popular name of the statement of financial position has been "balance sheet".

The fact that total assets are equal to the total of liabilities and stockholder's equity merely means someone has done good arithmetic. The equality says nothing of the quality of the information for investment (financial) decision making.

Assets

The accountant is very selective in what is considered to be a recordable asset. In general, to be eligible for consideration as an accounting asset, the item must have been purchased or obtained in an economic transaction. Although intangible assets may be recorded when an entire firm is purchased, more generally expenditures for intangible (e.g., research and development) assets are recorded as expenses. An expenditure is more likely to be recorded as an asset if the resulting item acquired can be seen and touched. Unless the item that is purchased is tangible, the likelihood of it being considered an asset is decreased considerably.

Another accounting convention is that cost is the basis of recording the asset. However, there are exceptions to this convention. For example, in cases where the current market value of inventory is less than cost, the firm may choose to apply "the lower of cost or market" rule to determine the basis of recording the asset. Also, we may have problems in determining the cost of assets. For example, we have measurement problems when the product is a joint product (as with determining the cost of a pork chop obtained as one of many products from a pig), when the value of the asset decreases through use (as with an automobile that is used on salty roads), or when the value of the asset increases through time (as with trees that are growing). In any of these situations, reports prepared by several accountants are apt to differ considerably, and the recorded cost is apt to be very different than the economic value of the asset.

The more frequently encountered asset classifications and the bases that are most frequently used in preparing balance sheets are as follows:

Asset Item	Basis of Recording
Cash or bank deposits	The face value.
Marketable securities (frequently readily marketable governmental securities	The lower cost of market. Some marketable securities are recorded at market value.
Accounts receivable	Face value less an adjustment for expected uncollectibles and for the timing of collection.

(Continued)

(*Continued*)

Asset Item	Basis of Recording
Inventories	The lower of cost or market (but cost may be measured in a variety of ways). With LIFO (Last-In, First-Out), the lower of cost or market cannot be used.
Investments in other firms	The lower of cost or market, or cost, or cost adjusted for the firm's equity in earnings since the acquisition of the stock.
Plant and equipment	Cost less accumulated depreciation, that is, cost reduced by a measure of the deterioration of the asset.
Goodwill and other intangibles	Cost reduced by an amortization amount where the goodwill was acquired in the purchase of another firm, but frequently goodwill is recorded at a nominal amount or not recorded at all.

It should be noted that the primary basis of recording each of the above items is objective evidence of the type associated with an explicit purchase price. If there is an adjustment from cost, it is generally in a downward direction to reflect a decrease in market value or the utilization of the asset. This is a reflection of the accountant's inclination to be conservative.

Any person analyzing the financial affairs of a corporation by inspecting a balance sheet should be aware of the information that is not presented, as well as the information that is contained in the report. The following information is frequently not given in the balance sheet:

a. The market value of marketable securities where market value exceeds cost.
b. The current market value of inventories.
c. The market value of investments in other firms.
d. The current value of long-lived assets (land, plant, and equipment), obtained in one of several ways — for example, by adjusting for

price-level changes using price indexes or by the use of appraisals. An estimate of economic value is not made.

e. The current value of natural resources. For example, the cost of drilling an oil well does not give an indication of the value of the oil in the ground.

f. The cost or value of research and development (R&D) expenditures or know-how. R&D expenditures must be treated as an expense of the period in which the expenditure is incurred; thus the asset R&D does not appear on the balance sheet.

g. The cost or value of training and education of management. These costs are treated as expenses.

h. The cost or value of past advertising expenditures (they are expensed as incurred).

Values are not generally used by the accountant in preparing a balance sheet. It should be noted that there are some situations where it would be difficult to record value even if we had the inclination. At what value should we record the value of a top-quality manager or the possession of good location for a store? A chemist may develop a new compound, but we do not know how to use it yet. What is its value?

Obviously there are some items where the accountant may use an objective measure of cost and still present a reasonable estimate of value. For example, a 90-day Federal government note may be recorded at cost, and the fact that the market value currently is a bit different from cost plus accrued interest may be ignored because the difference is not apt to be material given the short time till maturity. The materiality of the error is small (materiality enters into the treatment of many items).

There are many items that either are presented at amounts that are not useful or are not shown on the balance sheet at all. The investor must be particularly careful in appraising the balance sheet of a firm in an industry that involves natural resources (where factors of value are discovered or grown) or where the firm is engaged in a relatively large amount of research. In these areas, the adherence to cost and a failure to record intangible assets is apt to negate much of the usefulness of the financial reports of the firm's financial position and income.

Note that the term "liquidation value" was not used in this section, because the accountant assumes a "going concern", unless the firm is likely to be liquidated.

Sources of Assets

The asset sources are essentially of two types: liabilities and the amount of investment (explicit or implicit) of stockholders. In general, the measurement problems involving liabilities are much less than those with assets. Usually the liability takes the form of a legal contract, and thus the amounts to be paid are reasonably well defined. If the liabilities were all of a short-term value, the conventional liability measures would be very reliable.

Where the due date of the liability is a long time in the future, however, we have a problem of adjusting for the time value of money via a discounting procedure. It is likely that the book value of the long-term liability, the maturity or face value of the liability, and its current economic value will all be different. Thus the amount shown as the book liability for bonds payable may not be the current economic liability to the firm (they will be equal only if the current interest rate is the same as the interest rate at the time of issue, and if the security was issued at face value). The book value of the liability will differ greatly from the economic measure of the liability when there have been large changes in the interest rate and there is a long time until maturity.

A second problem with liabilities involves those liabilities associated with events that are still not completed. For example, a lawsuit may be pending, and the accountant must present a report without knowing the final judgment of the court. In this case, an estimate of the liability may or may not be made by the accountant, and the analyst must be sure that a reasonable estimate is made.

Sometimes there will appear in the sources side of a balance sheet a section containing "reserve" accounts. These reserves may have titles such as:

Reserve for contingencies
Reserve for possible loss in foreign investments
Reserve for lawsuits
Reserve for deferred taxes

or other titles that omit the term "reserve" but are equally ill-defined.

Reserves can be reclassified into subtractions from assets, additions to liabilities, or stockholders' equities. For example, the first two items are stockholders' equity items, the third is an expected liability, and the last is treated either as a subtraction from assets or a liability depending on the interpretation of the account. It is unfortunate when the term "reserve" is used with an inevitable attendant confusion. It is particularly confusing since a reserve account of the type we are discussing is not a "reserve" in the sense that most laymen would use the term. No liquid assets have been set aside for a contingency; thus the firm's ability to cope with an unfortunate event is not increased by the bookkeeping entry that gives rise to the account.

There are several liabilities that the accountant does not record in the balance sheet. The three most significant are debt of another corporate entity guaranteed by the firm, operating leases, and the debt of non-consolidated firms (firms that the parent owns stock in, but does not consolidate). Because these amounts may be large, the analyst must be prepared to make necessary adjustments when these situations exist.

The stockholders' equity section of a balance sheet is divided into several sections. One meaningful split occurs where there are preferred and common stockholders. We shall assume in this discussion that there is only common stock outstanding. The law requires that there be a split between the permanent capital (for example, common stock-par) and the capital available for dividends (for example, retained earnings). For many purposes, an investor is interested in the total sum of the stockholders' equity rather than the breakdown that we have described. On the other hand, creditors and stockholders may both be interested in knowing that the corporation cannot pay dividends because there is only permanent capital. This information should be disclosed.

The basic accounting equation (assets are identically equal to asset sources) may be redescribed as: the stockholders' equity is equal to the difference between assets and liabilities. This latter presentation is the basis of a form of statement presentation that shows a firm's financial position not as a balanced array, but rather in a step fashion with liabilities being subtracted from assets to obtain the stockholders' equity. It should be noted that an error in measuring assets or liabilities will also affect the measure of the stockholders' equity.

One of the more popular measures to a potential stockholder is the measure of book value per share (the total common stockholders' equity divided by the number of shares of common stock outstanding). Unfortunately, this measure is not any better than the measures of the assets and liabilities; thus it may be an unreliable indicator of value.

The Income Statement

The income statement is considered by many to be the most important financial statement. It is the basis of the earnings per share computation (total income of the firm divided by the number of common stock shares outstanding).

The leading problems associated with the measurement of income are:

1. The timing of the revenue recognition.
2. The matching of revenues and the expenses of earning the revenues.
3. The measurement of expenses.
4. The inclusion of special non-recurring items.

The accountant does not record revenue until it is realized. In general, this means that a market transaction has taken place that involves the corporation, and the corporation has received in exchange for the asset sold or service rendered either cash, a good accounts receivable, or some other readily measured asset (or a decrease in a liability).

The matching of expenses against the revenues that they help earn is particularly troublesome in a situation where there are assets being used which have a long life and are expected to earn revenues over several time periods. The decision as to how much of the cost of the asset should be allocated to each time period is a difficult problem. The measurement of the expense becomes even more difficult when there has been a significant change in the general price level that may cause the cost basis of recording the expenses not to reflect the current cost of using the assets.

The expense of using relatively short-lived assets may also have its measurement problems. For example, the use of inventory may give rise to an expense. How is the expense to be measured? What assumption should be made as to the flow of costs? The accountant may assume that the last goods purchased are sold first (LIFO) or that the first goods purchased are sold first (FIFO), or rather than make this choice, may use average costs. There are also other alternatives, and the choices of cost flow will affect the measure of the asset as well as the measure of the expense and thus the income.

The decision whether or not to include or exclude non-recurring items from the measurement of income is a troublesome one. For example, should an adjustment to Accumulated Depreciation (of past years) affect the income of the year? If this type of item is excluded from the income statement, it does not affect the income of this year, nor does it affect the income of any other year. This means that expenses may be understated for a period of years and then the firm may adjust the assets to take note of their decreased value, but not affect the income statement. Each year may show a profit, but the firm suffers an overall loss.

A possible solution to this problem is the so-called "clean surplus" rule. Following this rule, no entry of this type is made directly to retained earnings; instead, all items are run through the income statement. Although this procedure solves one problem, it creates another. The income of this period is affected by items that were caused by the past accounting procedures, and these items may have nothing to do with this accounting period except that they are recognized in this period. Such income measures, unless they are adjusted, are bad predictors of the next year's income. The "clean surplus" rule is generally accepted accounting practice.

It is common accounting practice to be consistent. Thus, a firm is not likely to follow one procedure one year and switch to another procedure in the next year, and in the following year switch back. A firm may change procedures, but it is not done lightly.

The measurement of a corporation's income is at best the result of many estimates. In some firms, the earning of revenue is an obvious event (for example, a cash sale at the local drugstore), but the revenue-producing event is frequently less obvious with a more complex firm. When is the revenue earned and when should it be recognized by a firm selling magazine subscriptions or by a firm building a ship? If a firm holds readily marketable securities that have increased in value, has a gain been earned and realized? Is it necessary to sell the security? General practice would say that it is necessary to sell the security, but this procedure might enable a management holding a portfolio of a large number of securities to determine its income by judicious choice of the securities that it sells in any time period, rather than by the dividend and market price changes of the period. This "cherry picking" gives rise to unreliable income measures.

The Change in Financial Position

In the past the term "funds statement" was generally applied to a statement of the sources and applications of working capital (that is, current assets less current liabilities), or to a statement of changes in cash. Now this type of statement is called a "statement of changes in financial position" and reports the change in the cash account.

If we define "current assets" to include items such as cash, marketable securities, inventories, and other items that are expected to be consumed in the coming 12 months, and if we define current liabilities to be debts coming due in the next 12 months, then the difference in current assets and current liabilities is one measure of the liquidity of the firm.

Among the sources of cash are funds generated by operations, the issuance of long-term debt or common stock, and the sale of long-lived assets. Among the uses of cash would be the retirement of long-term debt or common stock and the purchase of long-lived assets.

The "cash flow" for a firm (funds from operations) is a useful measure of a change in liquidity, as is the change in working capital. However, these measures are not substitutes for the measure of income. The statement of changes in financial position supplements the income statement. It does not replace it.

Consolidated Statements

It is common practice for the financial reports of corporations to be "consolidated" when one corporation owns other corporations. This means that when a parent company owns a given percentage of the shares of the subsidiary corporation, the financial affairs of several legal entities are combined into one set of financial statements. The advantage of this practice is that it simplifies the task of the analyst. Items that could result in double counting are eliminated, and the information is condensed into a form that makes the report much more usable.

There are two primary criteria commonly used to determine whether or not a subsidiary firm is to be included in consolidation:

1. The percentage of ownership.
2. The degree of control.

If the percentage of ownership is 50% or more, the corporation is likely to be consolidated. With a smaller percentage ownership or a lack of control, these characteristics might disqualify the firm from the consolidation process. If it is not consolidated, the investment would be recorded at cost or cost plus a proportion of the earnings of the subsidiary since acquisition. The proportion should be consistent with the percentage of ownership of the parent.

In recent years, the financial subsidiary (a captive finance company) has increasingly come into popularity. The financial subsidiary finances the purchases by customers of the parent's products. Generally the financial subsidiary will have a capital structure containing a large proportion of debt (more than the parent is likely to have). The parent is now required to consolidate the affairs of the financial subsidiary and the parent, even if the financial subsidiary has other activities than the financing of the parent's receivables. The primary argument against consolidation is that the nature of the business of the parent (a manufacturer) and subsidiary (a financial institution) are different. The consolidation of these affairs results in the inclusion of a large amount of debt associated with the financial subsidiary.

Another accounting problem arises at the time two corporations merge or one firm acquires a second firm. Assume the event can be handled as an acquisition of assets and assuming of liabilities (a purchase). With a purchase, only the retained earnings of the surviving corporation are carried forward. Following a strict interpretation of the entity concept (that is, the accountant is accounting for the corporate entity), we might start with no retained earnings, because the new corporation is in certain essential ways different from the old corporation. In practice, this latter interpretation is never applied.

Adjustments to Financial Statements

While analysis of financial statements is more of an art than a science, there are several steps that can be taken that will lead to better information:

1. The reports for the several years being reviewed should be made comparable. This may require adjusting the reports of several time periods so that they will be consistent with respect to accounting practices through time.
2. The reports of the several companies (or operating units) being analyzed and compared should be placed on as comparable a basis as possible.
3. Ratios, percentages, and key totals should be computed.

The first step in the analysis of financial statements is to place the reports of different companies and of different time periods on as comparable a basis as possible. This will frequently require the adjustment of both balance sheets and income statements.

The nature of the adjustments required will vary considerably. It may be that a change in the accounting procedure was made (such as changing from first-in, first-out, FIFO, to last-in, last-out, LIFO), for there are a wide variety of accounting procedures generally accepted and thus likely to be found in accounting reports. While the procedures may be generally acceptable to the accounting profession, it may still be necessary for the analyst to adjust the circulated reports in order to obtain more useful information.

The items which follow illustrate some of the more frequently encountered problems which give rise to the necessity for adjustments.

Adjustment of Assets

Inventories are a troublesome item because firms may be using, or have recently switched to, FIFO, LIFO, or average cost. The year of adopting LIFO will affect the value reported for LIFO inventory. Ideally, the inventories presented on the balance sheet should be at current cost, and the cost of goods sold should be placed on the same basis. While it is not presently acceptable for purposes of general reporting, the use of current market value would give significant information for decision-making.

The type and nature of the adjustments will vary from firm to firm and from industry to industry. We have mentioned a few items encountered but have not exhausted the possibilities. In general, the longer the asset items have been held by the firm, the more suspect is the original cost as an indication of value. An analogous statement is true of liabilities. Often, the amount recorded for a long-term liability will not indicate the economic impact of the debt now. For example, the effective liability of a $1,000 bond issued at par to yield 4% and with 20 years to maturity will not be $1,000 now if the current market interest rate is 16%. It is important that adjustments be made prior to the computations of ratios and percentages; otherwise, the computations lose much of their meaning. For some of the adjustments suggested above, the accounting report does not supply sufficient information about the firm. The investor may prepare estimates of the adjustments — or not make the adjustment, recognizing the fact that the information is somewhat less reliable because of the failure to make the adjustment.

Adjustment of Income Statements

Generally, the investor can assume that the revenues are recognized on the sales-accrual basis, but this should be checked in the case of construction firms or other firms engaged in contracts or products that will take a long time to fulfill or produce.

In accounting for the affairs of subsidiary corporations, the extent to which firms will include or exclude the affairs of the subsidiaries and prepare consolidated income statements will vary considerably. Subsidiaries are generally consolidated (that is, earnings of the subsidiary are considered as the earnings of the parent) based on the percentage of ownership but this is not always the procedure. If a subsidiary is not consolidated the liabilities of that subsidiary do not appear on the consolidated balance sheet, but they still would be relevant to the decision-maker.

Another problem in measuring income is the treatment of extraordinary items such as an adjustment of the long-lived asset account to take note of the fact that a plant is no longer economically useful. Write-offs of this nature may distort the result of this period's operations so that this period's unadjusted income is a poor basis for estimating next year's income. While items of this nature should be included in reporting the income of the period, its nature should be clearly disclosed. The investor trying to predict the future, based on results of operations of the past, would have to adjust the reported income for items of a non-recurring nature.

The cost of goods sold may require adjustment. The cost of goods sold is a function of the choice of inventory accounting method and thus must be placed on a basis comparable to the procedures of other firms if the firms are to be compared.

The depreciation accounting may require adjustment for several reasons. The use of accelerated depreciation may result in a reported depreciation expense in excess of the normal expense of using the fixed asset. The depreciation expense may be further distorted because the purchasing power of the dollar has changed considerably through time and the recorded cost of the asset may be a poor base for the computation of the depreciation expense. The relevance of cost-based depreciation will depend on how the information is being used.

Ratio Analysis

In order to present briefly the pertinent financial information of an organization, ratios and percentages are frequently used. No one ratio will give the entire picture, but they do tend to give indications, which assist considerably in appraisal of the financial position and operations of a corporation.

Measures of Liquidity — Quick and Current Ratios

Two common measures of liquidity, the acid test or quick ratio (liquid assets divided by current liabilities) and the current ratio (current assets divided by current liabilities). The two ratios differ in the degree of liquidity which they indicate. They are both useful indicators of the short-term ability of corporations to meet their obligations.

The two ratios have several weaknesses. For one, they ignore the rate at which funds are being used or generated by the firm. More importantly, the numerical values of the ratios can be changed by canceling assets against liabilities, or by paying off current liabilities at the end of the accounting period.

A partial answer to the above objections is to compute the net working capital (current assets minus current liabilities). The net working capital is not affected by cancellation of current assets against current liabilities or by payment of the current liabilities since both current assets and current liabilities are reduced.

What is a "good" current ratio? From the point of view of a creditor, the higher the current ratio, the better the creditor's position because a strong current ratio tends to increase the probability of being paid at the maturity of the debt. However, a good current ratio from the point of view of present stockholders is much more difficult to define. A low current ratio is relatively more risky than a high ratio, but it may mean that management is efficiently controlling its current assets and is working them more effectively than a company with a high current ratio. It may be that idle balances of cash are minimized and inventory controls are being used to reduce the amount of money tied up in inventory (consistent with a profit maximization objective). A high current ratio reduces financial risk, but it may also indicate that management is not exercising sufficient control over working capital items.

There is no completely correct or simple answer to the question of what is a good current ratio. A banker may require a strong current position and high current ratio. A stockholder may prefer that the resources be worked more intensively, even at the cost of increasing the financial risk. They may both be correct in the sense that their wishes are consistent with their investment objectives.

Long-Term Financial Liquidity

Instead of current liquidity, we can focus attention on the long-term financial liquidity of the firm. Non-current items would not be included in the analysis.

The first step is to relate the debt to the total sources of capital (or total assets) or relate the stockholders' equity to the total source of capital (a variation is to relate the stockholders' equity directly to the total debt). Among the ratios that are used are:

$$\text{Debt-Equity Ratio} = \frac{\text{Total Debt}}{\text{Total Assets}}$$

$$\text{Stockholders' Equity} - \text{Asset Ratio} = \frac{\text{Stockholders' Equity}}{\text{Total Assets}}$$

$$\text{Stockholders' Equity} - \text{Debt Ratio} = \frac{\text{Stockholders' Equity}}{\text{Debt}}$$

$$\text{Debt to Total Capitalization} = \frac{\text{Debt}}{\text{Debt} + \text{Stockholders' Equity}}$$

Instead of using the book figures, for some purposes we may want to use market quotations to compute the values of the stockholders' equity and debt. All the above ratios accomplish the objective of indicating the long-run financial structure of the firm and giving an indication of the firm's ability to withstand adversity over the long run (all other things being equal). But they are all ratios of "stocks" of assets and debt and ignore the flow of funds and earnings.

A measure that considers both the amount of debt and the flow of funds is:

$$\frac{\text{Total Debt} - \text{Current Assets}}{\text{Funds from Operations}}$$

Instead of subtracting current asset we can just subtract quick assets. A quick asset is more liquid than a current asset. For example, quick assets do not include inventories. For many purposes, it is desirable to relate the income of the period to average resources used during the period or to the average stockholders' equity. These returns on investment measure the effectiveness with which the resources are being used.

$$\text{Income} - \text{Asset Ratio} = \frac{\text{Income Before Interest}}{\text{Average Assets}}$$

$$\text{Income} - \text{Stock Equity Ratio} = \frac{\text{Income}}{\text{Average Stockholders' Equity}}$$

There are several difficulties with using these last two measures effectively. Most important, there are the problems of measuring income and investment. In addition, there is the fact that we are measuring a percentage (or ratio) that eliminates from consideration the size of the investment, thus, the measure may be misleading when we form an opinion of "goodness".

There is another important difficulty with the use of return on investment that arises in a variety of industries; the problem of assets not currently generating revenues. This problem is typified by firms that grow timber. Assume a timber company is growing 30 different stands of timber, and it wants to compute its return on investment. The investment of the company is in mills, roads, equipment, and timber. Assume that 29 of the timber stands are being grown for future harvesting. Should the cost (or the value) of these stands be included in computing the return on investment of the company (or of a division)? Growing timber should be excluded from the investment base in computing the return on investment of such a company. Each timber stand is an independent investment and will have its own return on investment when it is harvested.

Does this mean that the growing timber stands do not have a return during a year prior to cutting? In accordance with generally accepted accounting procedures, they do not have returns because no income is realized. It would be possible to consider the increase in value of each stand to be income and divide this increase in value by the beginning of the period value to obtain the return on investment during the period. Most firms would consider this gain to be unrealized. However, if the value of the growing timber is to be included in the denominator of the return on investment computation, it is also necessary to include the increment in value of the timber. The common procedure of dividing the operating income by the total investment in all timber land is not correct because it includes investment in the denominator that is not expected to earn any realized income for a number of years.

The same type of adjustment as that described for timber may have to be made for an oil company that owns a large oil reserve it does not intend to pump out for a number of years.

Including this oil in the investment base would distort the return on investment of the operating assets. It also applies to a manufacturing plant which has excess capacity expected to be used in the future.

Earnings of the Stockholder

The last line of a corporate income statement is sometimes labeled "earnings of the stockholders", and sometimes "net income" (or variants of these terms). The first implies that there has been some change in the stockholders' well-being; the second indicates a change in the affairs of the corporation without any implication about what has happened to the wealth of the stockholders. An increment in the stockholders' wealth may occur when the firm makes earnings and the stock market reacts favorably but it is the stock price change and the cash dividend that give rise to stockholders' wealth changes. However, there is justification for labeling the last line on the income statement "earnings accruing to stockholders".

Computation of Earnings per Share

An important problem in the computation of earnings per share is related to the number of shares of stock that are committed but are not yet outstanding. Committed shares arise with stock options, warrants, convertible bonds, and convertible preferred stock. One solution is to base earnings per share on the number of the corporation's common shares outstanding plus the number of common shares reserved for the conversion of convertible preferred stock and convertible debentures and for warrants or stock option plans where there are shares granted to employees but the options have not yet been exercised. The numerator also has to be adjusted to reflect the exercise of the common stock options. A second possibility defining the other extreme is to divide the earnings by the actual number of common stock shares outstanding.

The first calculation implicitly assumes that all the shares will be issued, the second implicitly assumes that none of the shares will be issued. These are the two extreme possibilities.

It is possible to make more detailed adjustments. For example, consider outstanding stock options. If all or some of the options were exercised, the corporation would immediately receive cash from the purchase of these shares by the employees holding the options. The cash inflow value could be invested by the firm in capital projects and/or financial assets with some resulting return on investment per annum. There would be a corresponding increase in the corporation's reported net income. For example, if we assume a 15% return on investment, the income should be increased by 15% of the cash contribution of the stock options. In this example, 15% represents the assumed expected after-tax return on incremental investment.

It can be argued that each unit of convertible preferred, convertible debentures and stock options should be brought into the analysis as if they had been converted. This may not be a valid procedure. For instance, suppose that the value of a convertible security as a bond or preferred stock greatly exceeds the market price of the common stock they would be converted into. The securities will probably not be converted at this time and the stock option will not be exercised now. Nevertheless, there does exist potential dilution of the shareholders' position, which will become a reality if the firm's situation becomes more prosperous. It would be possible to adjust for the probability of non-conversion or exercise.

Reporting for a Conglomerate

Rational investors want to know the type of firm in which they are investing. Since conglomerates engage in a wide range of business activities, the accountant supplies a breakdown of financial information by type of business activity, so that the investor can evaluate the importance of the several segments of the business enterprise to the reported earnings. Investors might have one point of view if they are investing in an electronics firm, and another point of view if the "electronics" firm is deriving 70% of its revenue and 80% of its income from a division manufacturing steel. Contemporary risk analysis requires as an input for knowledgeable investment decision making how the returns of the investment are correlated with a market portfolio return. To accomplish this risk analysis the investors need to know how much the several operating divisions earned and their sales. Unfortunately, for a person wanting exact numbers, any conglomerate will have a large number of costs that are joint to several operating divisions, thus the income attributed to each division will reflect a somewhat arbitrary cost allocation. This situation can be solved by showing the direct earnings before the deduction of joint costs and then the deduction of the joint costs.

There is no question that the presentation of one set of corporate data (say on a consolidated basis) for a conglomerate does not supply enough information to an investor who wants to make an informed risk analysis. At a minimum a break-down of income by types of business is needed (this information is supplied).

Buying Common Stock

What do Real World Investors Consider?

It is dangerous to suggest that we understand exactly what information real world investors consider when they analyze a common stock for purchase.

However, there are several factors that they certainly should consider, and it is likely that they do consider. We will consider each factor briefly.

Current Price/Earnings Ratio

While it is convenient to divide the last calendar year's earnings by current market price, a slightly improved calculation is to use the earnings of the last four quarters divided by the current market price. This gives an estimate of the relationship of current earnings power compared to current market price.

Before using the P/E ratio intelligently to evaluate a security we would have to estimate the rate at which we expect the earnings to grow. Unfortunately, the future growth rate can only be an estimate.

Current Price/EBITDA

Investors should be interested in the ratio of the stock price to earnings before interest, taxes, depreciation, and amortization. Some analysts prefer to use the ratio of price to cash flow from operations. Both measures give an indication of how the price relates to the current assets being generated by the firm. For some purposes (e.g., valuation of the common stock), one might want to deduct the after-tax interest expense and the expected tax expense.

Dividend Yield

Extend the current dividend rate into the next 12 months to determine the annual rate of dividends, and divide by the market price to obtain the dividend yield. This gives a measure of the expected cash return on investment. Since the growth in stock price is omitted, this measure is not to be confused with the "total return" one would earn by investing in stock.

Current Stock Price

The current stock price should be compared to the future expected price (but this latter measure is difficult to obtain). Lacking the future price, there is a tendency to compare the present price with past prices but such a comparison is of doubtful use since the future is important in determining value, not the past.

Price Volatility

What has been the volatility of the common stock price in the past? This gives us a measure of the past risk of the stock (the measure of the volatility should be about a trend line).

As long as we are interested in volatility, the fluctuations in earnings should also be measured.

The Beta

How correlated is the stock's return with the overall market's return? This measure is called the stock's Beta. There is a theory that Beta of a stock is a more important measure of risk than the volatility of the stock.

If a stock is more volatile than the market (for example, a 10% increase in the market return results in a 15% increase in the stock return and a 10% decrease in the market results in a 15% decrease in the stock) then this stock would be described as being very risky. A less risky stock would be one where the percentage change for the stock price (e.g., 10%) is less than that of the market (e.g., 15%).

Balance Sheet Ratios

All the balance sheet ratios (liquid asset ratio, current ratio, stock equity/debt, etc.) are of interest since they indicate liquidity as well as debt leverage. The absolute values and the sensitivity of these ratios for changes in different items are also of interest.

Footnotes to the Financial Statements

What do the footnotes tell us that lead to significant adjustments to the basic information that is used by the financial reporting services and news-papers? Footnotes and a knowledge of accounting can lead to significant adjustments to the financial data. Information about pension liabilities, debt guarantees, and similar information is relevant for evaluating a common stock.

The Story of the Company

What is there about the history of the company and its prospects that is of interest? Does the firm's research efforts and the nature of its product line give promise of large growth in earnings in the future? What are its plans for the future?

Earnings Trends

Consistent with the above is an inspection of the firm's earnings record and the trend in earnings. What is happening to sales, earnings before interest and taxes, and earnings after interest and taxes? What can we project for the future?

Special Information

Is there special information such as a raider buying shares of its stock? Or is there a special financial strategy such as the purchase of its own shares or a stable dividend policy?

Does the company have a large investment budget for the coming years that is likely to restrict dividend growth and even jeopardize the current level of dividends? Are there large capital expenditures required by law that will not increase revenues or decrease costs?

What Other Investments are Currently Held?

The value of a stock to an investor depends on the other investments currently held by the investor as well as the investor's current financial situation. Does the investor want cash yield or growth in stock price? Safety or risk?

Putting it Together

Putting all the above information together to arrive at an intrinsic value for the stock is not an exact science. The market price is easily obtained from reading the newspaper. The intrinsic value of a stock is to a large extent based on the future, and the future is not known to investors.

The Efficient Market

And then there is the efficiency market hypothesis. If the above explanations have led you to despair about your ability to evaluate systematically the intrinsic worth of a common stock, all is not lost. There is a theory that all the purchasers and sellers in the market act as a policing force that insures that all the information currently available is effectively taken into consideration by the market, and the market price of all common stocks reflect the information that is publicly available. In addition, the next period's price (for a short time in the future) is a random movement away from the current price, and one cannot make profits by trying to predict these changes in price. Instead of trying to analyze systematically the types of information described above, you can depend on others doing the job for you. At the extreme, you can throw darts at the *Wall Street Journal's* tabulation of common stock prices and make effective investment decisions by buying the stocks you hit.

There you have it. You can learn accounting and finance and estimate the intrinsic value of stocks. Or you can rely on others to move the stock price to where future value is reflected in the current price, and it does not make a difference which stock you buy (leaving out diversification and tax considerations).

It would be surprising if the current market prices of common stock did not in a reasonable way reflect available information. On the other hand, investors would not be acting in a responsible manner if they did not carry out at least a minimum of systematic analysis. If all investors assumed the market were efficient and did no analysis, the market would soon not be efficient.

There are three levels of investment decisions:

a. Which stock?
b. Extent of diversification?
c. What allocation between cash, debt, and stock?

Up to here, this chapter has been concerned with choosing which stock. Now we will focus on the extent of diversification. Consider the following table showing "Risk Reduction". With ten securities, you reduce 90% of the risk that can be reduced! With 100 securities, you reduce 99% of the risk that can be reduced. However, you reduce more risk if the securities have a relatively low correlation (connection).

Risk Reduction

Portfolio Variance as Fraction of Individual Security Variance

Number of Securities in the Portfolio	Percent of Max Risk Reduction
	$\dfrac{N-1}{N}$
1	0
2	1/2
10	9/10
100	99/100
∞	1

When can risk be reduced to zero? If the securities have outcomes that are independent of each other, or if the outcomes are negatively related. When one goes down, the other goes up.

Summary Remarks on Financial Analysis

The investor should look at the financial position of the firm as well as the past, present, and future operating results. Using ratios and other means of comparisons, conclusions may be drawn as to the firm's liquidity and its ability to continue operating in the face of adversity. It is important to recognize that in the long run the most important factor will be the firm's ability to make profits. Profits will tend to result in positive cash flow from operations and in favorable credit ratings from potential investors. A sound financial position will enable the firm to absorb temporary setbacks and allow it to attain its long-run profit potential. Thus, the investor must look at financial position, as well as the results of operations, for a more complete appraisal of the financial health of an organization.

The determination of the degree of liquidity of a firm is no simple task. In the long run, the liquidity may depend on the profitability of the firm, but whether the firm will ever survive to reach the long run will depend to some extent on its financial structure. It is necessary for both management and investors to make comprehensive computations indicating the degree of liquidity of a firm. These computations should not only be based on the actual results of the most recent accounting periods, but predictions should also be made into the future, and the effect of adverse business conditions should be taken into consideration.

Accounting reports are based on transactions or events that have already occurred. However, the value of a firm is based on the expectations of future events. It is the task of an investor to take the past accounting data and convert it into projections into the future, using not only the accounting information but also knowledge about the structure of the industry the firm is operating in and overall trends of the economy.

Although there are many valid criticisms that can be made about the current state of accounting practice, there are also many statements of praise that can be made. In general, we know the accounting basis of the financial statements, thus, we are aware of those situations where the information is not very usable. In those situations, we cannot use the information as the basis of making decisions. If we are analyzing the financial reports of an oil company, then we know that the long-lived asset measure shown on the balance sheet for oil is likely not to be equivalent with the value of the oil reserves. We may wish to know this latter information that is missing, but at least we are warned, and the informed reader should not be misled. Also, we know that certified financial statements are likely to be honestly prepared (barring very clever fraud). There may be differences of opinion as to how items should be presented, and all firms are not comparable, but at least we know that the figures for most industries are not likely to be rigged to suit the arbitrary purposes of management. On the negative side is the type of situation illustrated by the accounting for research and development. A decrease in research and development expenditures will increase the income of the present year, possibly at a cost of the income of future years that might otherwise have benefited from the research. Thus, the type of income manipulation is a more sophisticated variety that makes use of known loopholes in the accounting practice. Unfortunately, reducing research can have adverse economic effects (the arbitrary cutback in research to improve income of the present year is an example of adverse economic action).

Investments: Analysis of Common Stock

The following information is of interest:

a. Current market price.
b. Dividend yield (past 12 months and history through time).

c. Current price/earnings ratio.

d. Past market prices and fluctuations and forecast of future.

e. Relationship to other investments.

f. Earnings, current, past, and future.

g. Nature of the company's business, recent developments and future prospects, products and markets, practices.

h. Most recent quarterly results (earnings).

i. Balance sheet data: current ratio, debt/equity, etc.

j. Interest coverage (times earned).

k. Hidden liabilities (pension, leases, etc.).

l. Accounting practices (LIFO, depreciation, etc.).

m. Growth rates of earnings, dividends, etc.

n. Book value (the firm's stockholders' equity as measured by the accountants divided by the firm's shares of outstanding common stock).

o. Which market is it traded on? Liquidity of securities.

p. Strategy, operating and financial decisions of firm.

q. Capital structure.

r. Managerial compensation practices.

The Allocation

The allocation between stock and other investments, including cash is a difficult decision to make correctly. We know that for any 30-year time period since 1926, you are better off holding common stock than other security. However, there are three periods of 20 years in which the return from holding common stock did not do as well as debt.

We know that we have difficulty picking the moment of maximum stock market level and determining when the market has reached a bottom. We are not good allocating investments to maximize wealth.

However, based on past history, one should be 100% in stock if you believe history repeats itself, and you will hold the investment for at least 30 years after the worst market collapse. With less certain beliefs, you should not have 100% of your savings in stocks. Nor should you have 0% in stocks.

There can be a good firm with a good product, but it is a bad common stock investment (the stock price is too high) or the firm has "bad luck".

The investor who ignores the reports of the accountant because they are not exact forecasts of future value is making a grievous error. At best, reports of the accountant can never be better than a collection of estimates of values and events that are extremely difficult to measure. But these reports are useful markers.

We live in a world where the future is uncertain and the accountant is reporting events of the past. However, many useful projections into the future are based on past events. If we have a firm that in its best year has earned $2 per share, and if there has not been a special event that causes us to think the future history will be drastically different from the past, to ignore the accountant's measure of $2 and invest in the firm based on a $10 per share projected earnings for the coming year does not seem to be reasonable.

We can expect accounting practice to change in the future just as the accounting of the past has changed. There is room for improvement, but we start from a base that is reasonable and provides much useful information.

Questions

1. Assume ABC Corporation's balance sheet showed the following measures:

Cash	$ 5,000
Accounts Receivable	3,000
Inventories	12,000
Current Liabilities	10,000

   a. Compute the firm's quick ratio.
   b. Compute the firm's current ratio.

2. (Continue 1). The firm has $30,000 of total debt and funds from operations of $15,000.

   Compute some measures that give an indication of financial viability.

3. The following facts apply to the XYZ Company:

EBITDA =	$100,000
Interest	20,000
Taxes	30,000
Income	$ 50,000

   The firm's market capitalization (shares outstanding times market price) is $450,000.

   a. Compute the P/E ratio.
   b. Compute the Current Price/EBITDA ratio.

Part II
Tax Considerations

Tax factors should affect investment decisions. They are the most important consideration after the objective of achieving diversification.

First, taxes affect the type of security the investor should insert into the investment portfolio.

Secondly, taxes affect in what type of account we hold the securities. That is, should the securities be in a tax deferred account or a currently taxed account?

Third, taxes affect how one evaluates corporate financial decisions; thus they affect the selection of specific corporate securities.

Chapter 7

Stocks versus Bonds

We want to compare alternatives for an individual investments in corporate bonds and stock. Since the single most important variable for the analyst of a common stock investment is the price-earnings multiple, we will seek an equivalent calculation as the P/E multiple for a bond.

The discussion assumes that on a before tax basis the bonds can be better than the stock (a higher expected return). However, it is necessary to consider the two alternatives (buying stock compared to buying a bond) on an after-tax basis. It can be that the investment in stock is preferred, even with a lower expected return than debt, assuming the current tax laws.

The Bond "P/E"

We can compute the contractual yield (return) from investing in a bond (the actual yield earned may differ because of financial distress, early call or selling before maturity). Assume a bond contractual yield is 0.08. A measure comparable to a P/E for a stock is obtained by dividing 1 by the bond yield of 0.08:

$$\text{Bond ``P/E''} = \frac{1}{0.08} = 12.5 \text{ or equivalently } \frac{1,000}{80} = 12.5.$$

A \$1,000 bond selling at \$1,000 pays \$80 interest. This bond is selling at 12.5 times annual interest.

The P/E for Stock

A stock has three relevant flow measures:

1. Dividends

2. Earnings of Corporation (measured by accountants)
3. Cash flow from operations (after maintenance capital expenditures)

Assume a stock is selling for $100 (the price). It has:

$$\text{Dividends} = \$1$$
$$\text{Earnings} = \$4$$
$$\text{Cash flow} = \$10 \quad \text{(after maintenance cap-ex)}$$

The price–earnings ratio (P/E) is:

$$P/E = \frac{100}{4} = 25$$

When you buy, you want a low P/E. When you sell, you want a high P/E.

The Cash Flow Multiplier is:

$$\text{Cash Flow Multiplier} = \frac{100}{10} = 10 \text{ times.}$$

The Dividend Multiplier is:

$$\text{Dividend Multiplier} = \frac{100}{1} = 100 \text{ times.}$$

Using the P/E ratio for the stock (25), the stock is twice as costly as the $1,000 bond paying $80 of interest. Also, the bond has less risk if both securities were issued by the same corporation.

Consider the use of the stock's cash flow multiplier of 10 compared to 12.5 for the bond. But the cash flow multiple does not consider the interest and taxes that have to be paid, thus does not directly consider the net benefits to the stockholders.

The dividend multiplier of 100 leaves out the expected growth in stock price, thus cannot be compared to the 12.5 multiple of the bond where 12.5 measures all the expected benefits of the bond.

Thus we return to the P/E ratio of 25 as being the most useful summary measure relating common stock price to the benefit flow of the stock.

Next, we must consider the effects of income taxes on the choice between investing in stock or debt.

Tax Considerations

Assume the cost of equity, the return required (hoped for) by investors, (k_e) is 0.05 and the bond (debt) interest rate (k_i) is 0.06. These are also the two before tax expected returns for the two types of securities.

The tax rate of ordinary income (t_p) is 0.35 and the tax rate on dividend income (t_d) and capital gains (t_g) is 0.15.

$$t_p = 0.35, \quad k_e = 0.05, \quad k_i = 0.06, \quad (1 - t_p)k_i = 0.039$$

The number of years to be invested or the planning horizon (n) is 20 years.

$$n = 20 \text{ years}, \quad t_g = 0.15, \quad t_d = 0.15$$

Note that k_e, the stock required return before tax, is less than k_i, the cost of debt. Assume the investor can earn 0.039, after tax, investing in alternative investments.

The after-tax return from buying the 0.06 debt paying $60 of interest is:

$$(1 - 0.35)60 = \$39$$

$B(20, 0.039)$ is the present value of a 20-year annuity of $1 per year using a 0.039 annual discount rate and is equal to 13.7115. Assume the investor earns after-tax interest of $39 each year for 20 years and receives $1,000 at maturity.

$$PV = 39\,B(20, 0.039) + 1{,}000(1.039)^{-20}$$
$$= 534.75 + 465.25 = \$1{,}000$$

where $B(20, 0.039)$ is the present value of a 20-year annuity of $1 per year (received at the end of each year) discounted at an interest rate of 0.039. The annual after-tax cash flow from the bond is $39, therefore the present value of the after-tax cash flows for 20 years is $39\,B(20, 0.039)$ if the discount rate is 0.039. The $1,000 in the present value calculation is the payment of principle and is not taxed. The present value of the $1,000 is $1{,}000(1.039)^{-20}$.

When the after-tax interest amount divided by the principle is equal to the discount rate, the present value of the cash flow stream is equal to the principle, in this case $1,000.

$$\frac{39}{1,000} = 0.039.$$

Assume the investor buys $1,000 of the common stock where the corporation earns 0.05 per year on retained earnings and the corporation reinvests for 20 years. At the end of 20 years, the accumulation is distributed and the gain is taxed at 0.15.

$1,000(1.05)^{20} = $ $2,653.30 Value of $1,000 of new capital at time 20
$-1,000.00$ Tax Basis (cost of the stock for the investor)

1,653.30 Taxable Gain
$\times 0.15$ Tax Rate

$ 248.00 Tax

Net $= 2,653.30 - 248.00 = $2,405.30$

The common stock's value at time 20 is $2,405.30. The present value of the stock value is:

$$\text{PV of Stock} = 2,405.30(1.039)^{-20} = \$1,119$$

The following calculations for the common stock is equivalent to the above.

$$\text{PV of Stock} = [(1 - 0.15)1,000(1.05)^{20} + 0.15(1,000)](1.039)^{-20}$$
$$= (2,255.30 + 150)(1.039)^{-20} = \$1,119$$

where $(1 - 0.15)1,000(1.05)^{20}$ is the after-tax cash flow at time 20 if the stock grows at 0.05 per year.

Multiplying $1,000(1.05)^{20}$ by $(1 - 0.15)$ assumes a zero tax basis (protection against the tax) and $0.15(1,000)$ is the value of the $1,000 tax basis (cost of stock) at time 20.

Since $1,119 is larger than $1,000, with this set of assumptions the stock investment beats the debt investment. The gain would be larger if the corporate reinvestment rate (0.05) were larger. Also, the difference in dollar value is larger if we use future values rather than present values.

The following summarizes the above calculations.

Debt ($k_i = 0.06$)

Assume a 0.06, $1,000 bond is purchased for $1,000.

The after-tax interest flows are $(1 - 0.35)60 = \$39$.

$$\text{Future Value} = 39 \, \text{B}(20, \, 0.039)(1.039)^{20} + 1,000$$
$$= 1,149 + 1,000 = \$2,149$$

or

$$1,000(1.039)^{20} = \underline{\$2,149} \quad \text{Value of the debt at time 20.}$$

The present value is $2,149(1.039)^{-20} = \$1,000$
The present value of a \$1,000 investment in the debt is \$1,000.

Common Stock ($k_e = 0.05$)

$$\text{Before Tax Future Value} = 1,000(1.05)^{20} = \$2,653$$
$$\text{Tax} \qquad -248$$
$$\overline{}$$
$$\underline{\$2,405}$$

$$\text{PV} = 2,405(1.039)^{-20} = \$1,119.$$

The Indifference Rate for Debt

Continuing the above example, the after-tax value at time 20 for a \$1,000 investment in stock is \$2,405. It can be shown that this investment in common stock earns a compounding rate of 0.0448 per year (after tax).

What interest rate would a debt investment have to pay in order for the investor to earn 0.0448? Let k_i be the required debt rate, then if $t_p = 0.35$:

$$(1 - t_p)k_i = 0.0448$$
$$0.65 \, k_i = 0.0448$$
$$k_i = 0.0689$$

When the common stock earns (before tax) 0.05, for the investor to be indifferent, the debt would have to earn at least 0.0689 per year (before tax) with the given assumptions.

The debt required return would depend on the time horizon being assumed for the common stock. Also, we do assume that the common stock returns are taxed after 20 years. We could have assumed zero tax on the common stock at time 20.

Common Stock Dividends and Capital Gains

We want to compare the difference in returns on common stock when a company retains and when it pays a cash dividend.

Assume:

Capital gains tax rate $= 0.15$
Return (after tax) investors can earn $= 0.085$ (on alternative investments of comparable risk).
Return corporation can earn $= 0.10$ (before investor tax)
Investment horizon $= 15$ years
Corporation has $100 that it can invest or pay a dividend.
Tax on dividends $= 0.15$

Dividend

Assume the corporation pays a $100 dividend. The investor nets $85 and earns 0.085 per year for 15 years.

$$85(1.085)^{15} = \$289 \quad \text{Value of investment after 15 years}$$

Retention of $100 and then Capital Gain

The corporation reinvests $100 and earns 0.10 per year for 15 years and then the investor is taxed at 0.15. The after-tax value after 15 years is $355.

$$100(1.1)^{15}(1 - 0.15) = \$355$$

The corporation can earn 0.10 per year (after corporate tax). Retention by the corporation results in $355 and easily beats the dividend where the investor receiving the dividend accumulated $289.

If the time horizon is lengthened, the gap in the future values will widen. Also, if the tax rates on dividends and capital gains differ, this will also affect the magnitudes of the benefits and the conclusions.

Summary

Investments in common stocks lodged in a taxed account may tend to beat investment in bonds even if they have the same or lower before tax returns because of lower tax rates for dividends. But even if the tax rates were the same for investments in stock and debt, stock would still have the advantage of tax deferral if the corporation is retaining some of its earnings. Bond interest is taxable when it is paid (or more exactly, when it is earned).

It is also implied in one example that retention by the corporation is more desirable than a cash dividend as long as the corporation can earn a return larger than the return the investor can earn on equivalent risk securities in the market (after the investor's tax).

We have only considered investments in taxed accounts. If one wants some debt in the investment portfolio, locating the taxable bonds in a tax deferred account is sensible. Tax exempt bonds (e.g., munis) should be placed in taxed accounts.

Questions

1. A $1,000 bond selling at $1,000 pays $50 annual interest.
   A stock is selling at $40 and is earning $2 per share.
   Which security offers the better return?
2. Assume bond interest is taxed at 0.35 and dividends on common stock
   at 0.15. Assume bonds are yielding 0.06 interest (before tax).
   To obtain the same after-tax cash flow, the dividend yield would have
   to be _____ %.
3. (Continue 2). If the dividend yield from common stock is 0.05 and 0.0425
   after tax, what interest does a bond have to pay to offer the investor the
   same 0.0425 return?
4. (Continue 2). The corporation can pay a $100 dividend and the investor
   can earn 0.10 (after tax) on the investment for one year.
   Alternatively, the firm can retain the $100, earn 0.12 for one year and
   then pay a dividend (investment plus earnings).
   What is the investor's preference?
5. (Continue 2 and 4). Is it reasonable that the investor only earns 0.10
   when the firm earns 0.12?

Chapter 8

Taxed and Tax Deferral Accounts

Stock returns in a taxed investment account are normally taxed in the U.S. at a 0.15 rate. In a tax deferral account, they are taxed at a maximum rate of 0.35. Is it advantageous to transfer funds invested in stock from a tax deferred account to a taxed account?

This chapter's Appendix 1 shows a numerical example where it is not desirable to transfer from a tax deferral investment account to a taxed investment account. Appendix 2 shows that if the tax basis in the tax deferred account is zero, it is not desirable to withdraw funds early. However, because the rules and facts change, the value of the two alternatives should be calculated. Consider the following factors:

Factors Leading to Retention in Tax Deferred Account

a. A large tax (low tax basis) on withdrawal.
b. A large difference in return earned on investments in tax deferral accounting compared to return earned on taxed account (the difference can be caused by taxes).
c. The income is taxed at the same rate in both types of accounts.
d. The time horizon is long until the funds are converted to consumption.
e. A reduction in tax rates is expected.

Factors Leading to Transfer to Taxed Account

a. No tax or low tax on transfer. The transfer is protected from taxes (a large tax basis).
b. Small difference in returns earned in the two types of account.
c. The income on the taxed account is taxed at a lower rate.
d. Time horizon is short until funds are converted into consumption.
e. An increase in tax rates is expected.

The most likely outcome of calculations will be to keep funds invested in a tax deferred account rather than to transfer them (see the Appendices 1 and 2). The most important determinant is the tax imposed on the transfer from the tax deferral account. The primary factor that might swing the decision to transfer are a lower tax rate on capital gains and dividend income on securities in a taxed account. Thus the taxed account has a tax advantage on incremental incomes.

Is Using a Tax Deferral Account Desirable?

First, we will assume that incomes of both a tax deferral and a taxed account are taxed at the same rate but at different times. In this situation, the tax deferral account wins handily.

Tax deferral accounts have a second advantage. They may avoid immediate income taxes on the funds invested. The following accounts avoid the income tax at time of investment on the amounts invested.

(401 K) (a form of retirement savings account)
IRAs (some types avoid the income tax, but not all)
Keough plans, etc. (a Keough plan enables a self-employed worker to set up a retirement account and avoid immediate taxes).

With a 0.35 tax rate, $100 that goes into an eligible (401 K) account immediately saves $35 of taxes, thus $100 is invested. If the same $100 were to be invested in a taxed account, the $100 would immediately shrink to $65 because of the $35 tax. Some investors do not invest the maximum amount allowable under the law in their (401 K) accounts because they do not have the money. If one can borrow at normal home equity rates, it is going to be desirable to borrow and make the maximum investment assuming the investor is in a relatively high tax bracket. Saving the tax on the investment is powerful as is the subsequent investment income earned and accumulating on a before tax basis. It is always desirable to do the arithmetic to determine if it is desirable to borrow the funds to invest in a (401 K) account.

Roth IRA's have special tax features. The funds going into a Roth IRA have been taxed, and this is a disadvantage compared to other tax deferral accounts. But "qualified" distributions (investment and earnings) from a Roth are not taxed. Unfortunately, the investment contributions per year are limited. In addition, if your adjusted gross income is too large you cannot make contributions to a Roth. But we can expect that new tax deferral plans will be introduced by the Federal Government. Remember that such plans should be evaluated on an after-tax basis; but they tend to be desirable investment alternatives.

A qualified distribution from a Roth IRA is made when the participant has reached age 59 $1/2$, is disabled or dies. In addition, the distribution has to be made at least five years after the participant made the first contribution to the Roth plan.

A non-qualified plan is taxed to the extent that the distribution exceeds the amount invested that has already been taxed.

Example

Mr. Jones can borrow $100 at 0.08. Assume the $8 of interest cannot be a tax deduction. The debt proceeds can facilitate a $100 investment in a tax deferral account earning 0.08. The $100 investment would save $35 of taxes at time zero.

	Time		Interest Rates
	0	**1**	
Borrow	+100	−108.00	0.08
Investment	−100	+108.00	0.08
Taxes Saved	+35		
Taxes Paid (0.35×108)		−37.80	
Total	+35	−37.80	0.08

The transactions are equivalent to borrowing money at a 0.08 interest rate. Mr. Jones should borrow to invest the $100 in the tax deferral account if he is willing to borrow at 0.08. The above calculations assume the interest on the debt do not lead to a tax deduction. If more than 0.08 can be earned on the $100 investment, this will enhance the borrowing alternative.

Stock Placed in Taxed or Taxed Deferral Accounts

Assume a situation where the investor has decided to invest in stock but has to decide whether to place the investment in a taxed account or a tax deferral account.

If an amount invested in the tax deferral account leads to an immediate reduction in the current income tax from a rate of 0.35 to 0.15 for common stock earnings, then the taxed account beats the taxed deferral account for short horizons.

Example

Let t_d be the tax rate on dividends and t_p the tax rate on ordinary income. $t_d = 0.15, t_p = 0.35$, investments earn 0.10 (before investor tax) and 0.085 if invested in taxed account. Amount to be invested is $1,000 (before tax) and $650 after tax.

If the $650 of stock is in a taxed account, after one year the investor has:

$$650(1.085) = \$705.25$$

If the $1,000 of stock is in a tax deferral account and saves $350 of immediate income taxes, the investor has after one year:

$$
\begin{array}{ll}
1,000(1.10)^1 = & \$1,100 \\
\text{Tax on } \$1,100 & \underline{385} \\
& \overline{\$715}
\end{array}
$$

The advantage of the tax deferral account increases as the time horizon is lengthened.

But suppose the $1,000 does not reduce immediate taxes (as with a Roth account) and only $650 is invested. For short-term periods, the taxed account is better than the tax deferral account. The tax deferred values are:

$n = 1$

Investment	$650.00
Earnings	65.00
	$715.00
Tax (0.35×65)	22.75
	$692.25

The $650 in the taxed account grows to $705.25 (see above), thus the taxed account is preferred to the $692.25 if $n = 1$.

$\underline{n = 20}$

Assume $1,000 is invested on a tax deferral basis.

$$1,000(1.10)^{20} = \qquad \qquad \$6,727$$

Taxable income	5,727	
Tax rate	$\times 0.35$	2,004
Net		$4,723

With the taxed account we have:

$$650(1.085)^{20} = \$3,323.$$

If $n = 20$, tax deferral is better than the taxed account.

$\underline{n = 40}$

$$1,000(1.10)^{40} = \qquad \qquad \$45,259$$

Taxable income	44,259	
Tax rate	$\times 0.35$	15,491
Net		$29,768

With the taxed account we have:

$$650(1.085)^{40} = \$16,986.$$

With long lives the tax deferral account is to be preferred.
Conclusion: Do the calculations.

A Traditional IRA

If funds in an IRA are withdrawn before the owner reaches 59 $1/2$, there is a 10% tax penalty (there are some exceptions that will eliminate the penalty).

No contributions may be made to the IRA after the owner reaches 70 $1/2$. There are minimum distribution rules (the rules keep changing). On the one hand, the Federal Government does not want to have the totals in IRAs to be too large (thus limiting the contributions and having minimum distributions). On the other hand, the tax advantages of IRAs are structured to encourage the creation and expansion of the amounts invested. How evil would it be to have fewer limits on what people can do? Someone in the government should define the objectives and how best to achieve them. Now there are too many mixed signals.

Withdrawals

Is it better to withdraw $100 from a Roth or a traditional IRA if funds are needed for consumption? The tax rate is 0.35.

If there is a $100 eligible withdrawal from a Roth we have:

$$\text{Net} = \$100$$

If there is an eligible $100 withdrawal from a traditional IRA the investor nets

$$\text{Net} = 100(1 - 0.35) = \$65.$$

The withdrawal seems to be desirable from the Roth. But remember that the total future proceeds from the Roth are exempt from Federal taxes and the proceeds from the IRA are subject to taxes. If the investment horizon is longer than an immediate withdrawal for the remaining investment it might be desirable to leave the investment funds in the Roth.

Assume that with a 0.10 earnings rate, after ten years both funds with $100 of investment will have $259.39. After tax with a traditional IRA (tax rate = 0.35) the investor will net $168.59 and with a Roth $259.39. The Roth has an advantage of $259.39 - 168.59 = \$90.80$.

Liquidating the Roth would save $35 of taxes at time 0. Invested for ten years at 0.10, the $35 grows to $90.80. There is indifference. But if the tax savings of the Roth liquidation earn less than 0.10 (this is a reasonable forecast), liquidating the Roth to save $35 of taxes would be an inferior strategy.

Example

We want to compare a tax deferral account (such as a retirement or IRA account) versus a taxed account.

The investor earns $100 (before tax). The tax rate is 0.35. On investment income, the investor earns 0.10 (before tax) and 0.065 (after tax). There is one year until consumption:

Tax Deferral: Future Value $= 100(1.10)(1 - 0.35) = \$71.50$
Taxed Account: Future Value $= 65(100)(1.065) = \$69.225$

If dividends are taxed at 0.15 and the after-tax investment return is 0.085 for the taxed account, we have:

Taxed Account: Future Value $= 65(100)(1.085) = \$70.525$

The tax deferral account with \$71.50 wins the contest. But is it reasonable that the investor earns a lower return in the taxed account than in the taxed deferral account? Since the investment income is taxed currently in the taxed account, the expected return is lower.

The above two examples were for one year. A longer time horizon will widen the spread between the outcomes.

Roth 401 (K)

The 2003 tax revision included a Roth plan provision that did not go into effect until January 2006. The contributions to the type of Roth 401 (K) are after tax but there are no income limits to be eligible. The maximum 2006 limit is \$15,000 unless you are 50 years old or older. If the investor is older than 50 years, the limit goes up to \$20,000 (the plain **401 (K)** account has the same limit, but the limit is before tax).

The Roth 401 (K) is scheduled to expire in 2010 unless Congress passes a new provision.

We will compare an investment in a plain **401 (K)** and a Roth 401 (K). The results are somewhat surprising.

A Tax Deferral Account (401 (K))

An investor has \$100. If placed in the tax deferral account (a 401 (K)), it will save \$35 of taxes. After n years, the entire amount will be taxed at 0.35. Funds invested earn r.

$$FV = 100(1 + r)^n (1 - 0.35) = 65(1 + r)^n$$

Roth 401 (K)

Instead of the tax deferral account, assume the \$100 is taxed and \$65 is placed in a Roth 401 (K). The future value is:

$$FV = 65(1 + r)^n$$

and no tax on any of the proceeds at time n.

Note that the two future values are equal, if no tax rate changes are expected, and if the amounts invested are as shown.

The Roth is preferred if tax rates are expected to be higher in the future.

Tax Efficient Funds

There are mutual funds that adopt a strategy of being tax efficient. While not all funds that advertise being tax efficient are actually tax efficient, we will assume that we have found a mutual fund that is tax efficient.

A critic of such funds once stated "Their advantage is not real. It is only time value." It is true that it is time value but time value is extremely important and is real.

Assume a fund has $6,666.67 of capital gains and $1,000 of potential tax. The capital gains tax rate is 0.15. The fund can earn 0.10 on reinvested capital.

Time	Present Value of Tax (0.10)	Saving of Deferral	Saving Percentage
0	$1,000	0	—
1	909	91	0.091
10	386	614	0.614
20	149	851	0.851
30	57	943	0.943
50	9	991	0.991

Each year has its own present value of taxes, and potential savings. As shown by the above table, the time value of money can, with deferral of 50 years, reduce the tax cost by 0.991.

What are the Facts?

It is clear from the calculations that it is desirable to invest in a (401 K) account and investment may be desirable even if you have to borrow in order to invest. But the facts as to participation are discouraging. Seventy percent of young workers (18 to 25) do not invest in (401 K) accounts even if they are eligible. While older workers do somewhat better, their record of investing is not good. Many people do not have an adequate understanding of compound interest.

Consider the following table showing the future value of saving $5,000 a year and reinvesting at a 0.10 interest rate.

Years of Saving (Years to Retirement)	Future Value of $5,000 per Year Saved
5	$30,526
10	79,687
20	286,375
40	2,212,963

In addition, assume $5,000 placed in a (401 K) will save $1,500 a year of taxes (assuming a 0.30 tax rate).

Years of Tax Savings	Future Value of Tax Savings
5	$9,158
10	23,906
20	85,913
40	663,889

The above calculations assume that the tax rate is zero at time of retirement. If the tax rate is t, then multiply the numbers in the tables by $(1 - t)$.

Obviously, the time until retirement from the first time of saving affects materially the amount the worker will have at retirement. Delaying the time of first saving is not recommended.

Stocks or Bonds

Let us assume that the need for diversification dictates some stock and some bond investments. Which should be located in taxed accounts and which in tax deferred accounts?

As long as stock dividends and capital gains are taxed at 0.15 and ordinary income at 0.35, the stocks have an advantage compared to bonds in taxed accounts. Stocks in a taxed account have a tax advantage compared to bonds in a taxed account.

Bonds have less of a tax disadvantage in a tax deferred account.

The recommendation is clear if it has been decided to invest in both stocks and bonds and if both are taxed, tax deferral accounts are to be used for taxable bonds. We conclude:

Stocks go first into the taxed account.

If more investment in stock is desired and if there is capacity, then the additional stock goes into the tax deferral account.

Bonds go first into the tax deferral account if they are bonds that are taxed. Tax exempt bonds should go into taxed accounts.

If more bonds are desired and the tax deferral accounts are full, then probably tax exempt bonds are more desirable than taxable bonds in the taxed accounts. The after-tax returns should be compared.

If the tax laws change or are different than the current U.S. laws, the applicable rates should be used to determine the optimum strategy.

Mutual Funds

Mutual funds have the advantage of giving the investor a large amount of diversification. One of the disadvantages is the fees charged for management and for transactions. But the main disadvantage of many mutual funds is that capital gains tend to be realized. This creates a capital gains tax that with an alternative investment strategy might have been avoided.

One solution is to use a tax deferred account to house the mutual fund. A second solution is to choose mutual funds that are tax efficient. Make sure these funds are actually tax efficient and not merely advertised as being tax efficient.

Summary

The conclusion is that if funds are invested in a tax deferred account they should probably be left there until it is time to consume the accumulation or the law requires removal. A desire to obtain cash to make a gift would result in an exception to this rule as would different assumptions. For example, if the tax basis of the tax deferred assets is very large, this would make it feasible for the correct decision to be a transfer to a taxed account.

Appendix 1

Is a Transfer from a Tax Deferral Account Desirable? A Numerical Example

Let

t_p be the tax rate on debt interest

t_g be the capital gains tax rate

t_d be the tax rate on dividends

n be years of time horizon

r_p be the return earned by investor (after tax)

r be the return earned by investor (before tax)

Assume $100 in a tax deferred account and that:

$$t_p = 0.34, \quad t_g = t_d = 0.15, \quad n = 10, \quad r = 0.10, \quad r_p = 0.085$$

For any time horizon, funds kept in the tax deferred account beat transferring the investment to a taxed account. This conclusion is independent of the tax rate on dividends, but does depend on other assumptions. For example, both of the Appendices assume the tax basis of the investment in the tax deferred account is zero. Also, no tax rate changes are expected in the future.

Keep the Investment in Retirement Account (Earn 0.10)

FV is the future value. The total amount is taxed at a 0.34 rate.

$$FV = 100(1 - 0.34)(1.10)^{10} = \$171$$

This assumes the tax basis of the $100 investment is zero.

Transfer to Taxed Account and Retain

The $100 is taxed at 0.34 so that only $66 is available for investment in the taxed account. The tax basis for the taxed account is $66.

$$100(1 - 0.34)(1.10)^{10} = \quad \$171$$

$$\text{Tax } (0.15) \quad -26$$

$$\$145$$

$$\text{Tax Basis } (66)(0.15) \quad +10$$

$$\text{Future Value} \quad \$155$$

Should funds be withdrawn from a tax deferred account? Assume the initial tax basis of the accumulation is zero. The $66 of investment earns 0.10 per year. The new tax basis is $66. Transfer is not desirable.

If the funds (X) are left in the tax deferral account, earn r, and are withdrawn at time n and taxed at a 0.34 rate, we have for $r = 0.10$ and $n = 10$:

$$FV = X(1 - t_p)(1 + r)^n$$
$$= 100(1 - 0.34)(1.1)^{10} = \$171.$$

If the funds (X) are withdrawn immediately, taxed at t_p, and invested to earn r for n periods and then taxed at a rate of t_d:

$$FV = X(1 - t_p)(1 + r)^n(1 - t_d) + X(1 - t_p)t_d$$
$$FV = 66(1.10)^{10}(1 - 0.15) + 66(0.15)$$
$$FV = 145.51 + 9.90 = \$155.41$$

In the first equation, X is withdrawn from tax deferral and it is taxed so we multiply X by $(1 - t_p)$. In the numerical example, we have:

$$X(1 - t_p) = 100(1 - 0.34) = \$66.$$

The $66 earns 0.10 for ten years:

$$X(1 - t_p)(1 + r)^n = 171.19.$$

The $171.19 is then taxed at $t_d = 0.15$:

$$X(1 - t_p)(1 + r)^n(1 - t_d) = 171.19(1 - 0.15) = 145.51.$$

The term $X(1 - t_p)t_d$ recognizes that the tax basis is $X(1 - t_p)$. The value of the tax basis is:

$$X(1 - t_p)t_d = 66(0.15) = \$9.90.$$

It is desirable to leave the funds in the tax deferred account with these facts. The reinvestment rates (r) in the above examples can be changed.

Appendix 2

Appendix 1 shows that

$$FV_1 = X(1 - t_p)(1 + r)^n$$

for keeping the funds in the tax deferral account and

$$FV_2 = X(1 - t_p)(1 + r)^n(1 - t_d) + X(1 - t_p)t_d$$

if the funds of X are withdrawn immediately.

When is immediate withdrawal desirable? If $t_d = 0$, then immediate withdrawal is equally desirable to keeping the funds in the tax deferral account.

Rearrange terms for FV_2:

$$FV_2 = X(1 - t_p)(1 + r)^n - X(1 - t_p)(1 + r)^n t_d + X(1 - t_p)t_d$$

$$FV_2 = FV_1 - X(1 - t_p)[(1 + r)^n - 1] t_d$$

The second term is likely to be positive and reduce FV_2 so that it is smaller than FV_1.

Questions

1. Mr. Smith can borrow at 0.06 and investments are expected to earn 0.10 in a tax deferral account. Mr. Smith's tax rate is 0.35.

   Assume Mr. Smith borrows $1,000 to pay for the $1,000 placed in a tax deferral account. The interest on the funds borrowed does not result in a tax deduction.

   Is this borrowing and investing desirable?

2. The investor has decided to invest $1,000 in a tax deferral (can earn 0.10) or a taxed account (can earn 0.085). The tax deferral account will result in an immediate $350 tax saving. The tax rate on common stock earnings in a taxed account is 0.15.

   Which account should receive the $1,000? Do a one-year analysis.

3. An investor saves $10,000 a year and earns 0.20. After two years ($10,000 is saved three times)

Time	Cash
0	10,000
1	10,000
2	10,000

   At time 2, the investor will have $_____.

4. (Continue 3). At time 3, the investor will have $_____.

5. (Continue 3 and 4). Assuming the invested funds can earn 0.20 and four payments are made into the investment account, the investor can spend $_____ each year for perpetuity (first payment at time 5).

Chapter 9

Dividends versus Share Repurchase

Imagine the stock of two companies (A and B) where the earnings forecasts for both companies are identical. Both companies are earning $10 per share. Company A is paying a cash dividend of $6 per share. Company B is paying a zero cash dividend, but is using $6 per share to repurchase shares of its stock. All investors paid $100 per share for the stock.

Would you buy the shares of A or B? Assume you pay a 0.15 tax on both dividends and capital gains.

Many investors would prefer A with the $6 dividend. But we will do some calculations to evaluate the choice of A.

Assume the two stocks are initially both selling at $100 per share and the market capitalization of both companies is $1,000,000 (there are 10,000 shares outstanding for each company). An investor currently owns 1,000 shares of each company. She is taxed at a rate of 0.15 on dividends.

Company A is paying a $6 dividend per share or $60,000 in total. After the $60,000 dividend the market cap is reduced to $940,000 (this is correct if the market valued the dividend at $60,000) and the new market price after the dividend is paid is $\frac{940,000}{10,000} = \$94$ per share.

The investor owning 1,000 shares now has:

Dividend (Cash)	$6,000	
Tax (0.15)	-900	$5,100
Stock Price	$94	
Shares	$\times 1,000$	94,000
	Total Value	$99,100

The investment's initial value for 1,000 shares was $100,000. The decrease in value of the cash and stock owned by the investor is equal to the $900 income tax paid.

Now let us assume firm B spends the $60,000 on share repurchase instead of a cash dividend. The firm buys 600 shares of its stock at $100 per share. The new stock price (after repurchase) is:

$$\text{B's New Price} = \frac{1,000,000 - 60,000}{10,000 - 600} = \frac{940,000}{9,400} = \$100$$

There is no change in the stock price of B and the investor owning 1,000 shares still has a $100,000 investment. The investor who does not sell pays zero tax (has zero taxable income).

But now assume the investor has a desire to have $6,000 cash so the investor sells 60 shares and retains 940 shares. The tax basis for the investor for the 60 shares sold is $6,000 so there is no capital gains tax. The investor now has:

Cash		$6,000
Stock Price	$100	
Shares	× 940	94,000
	Total Value	$100,000

With a dividend, the investor had $5,100 of cash and owned 10% of the stock worth $99,100 in total (cash and stock). With share repurchase the investor had $6,000 of cash and owned 10% of the shares of stock $\left(\frac{940}{9,400} = 10\%\right)$. Share repurchase wins by saving the $900 of taxes paid on the $6,000 of cash dividends.

Now assume the tax basis of the stock is $0, so that the investor pays a 0.15 capital gains tax of $900 on the $6,000 capital gain. Now the investor has:

Cash		$5,100
Stock Price	$100	
Shares	× 940	94,000
	Total Value	$99,100

This outcome ties the result with a cash dividend. But of course the tax basis is not likely to be zero and if it is zero, the investor may decide not to sell any shares. Not selling any shares with the firm repurchasing 600 shares the investor will again have $100,000 of value (1,000 shares worth $100 each).

In the above example, from the viewpoint of the taxed investor, share repurchase beats or ties the cash dividend. More generally, the probability of share repurchase, beating the dividend is almost certain.

There are several results of the company's distribution policy that we have not considered. The market might prefer the cash dividend and increase the stock price of firm A paying the dividend even though taxed investors are worse off with the dividend than with an equal dollar amount of share repurchase.

Secondly, with firm B the increased demand for the stock (the company buying shares) might increase the stock price above $100. Or the market might rationally like the share repurchase strategy and increase the stock price because of the firm's share repurchase strategy.

While the above price changes might occur, we cannot easily quantify the consequences, so we will not attempt to bring these factors into the analysis.

The Option to Retain

With a cash dividend, all stock investors receive cash (and are taxed). With share repurchase, the investor has an option to increase her percentage of ownership in the firm (and avoid income taxes) by not selling. This option not to sell has value to the investor owning the stock.

Equal Tax Rates

Assume the tax rates on dividends and capital gains are equal. Does it make a difference whether the firm's distribution policy leads to dividend income or capital gains?

Since the investor with the prospective capital gain can delay or eliminate the gain by not selling the stock, the corporate strategy (share repurchase) leading to capital gains is preferred to the strategy where the investor is taxed currently on dividend income. Also with share repurchase the investor's tax basis for the stock sold reduces the taxes paid. Even though dividends and capital gains are taxed at the same rate, the tax effects are different because the timing and tax calculation rules are different.

Advantages of Share Repurchase

There are several advantages of share repurchase to both the taxed common stock investor and to the corporate managers. These include:

1. Flexibility (to corporation deciding when to buy and disburse cash).
2. Tax basis protection (for the investor. Not all cash flow is taxed, only the gain).
3. Ineligible dividends (differential tax rates. Not all dividends are taxed at 0.15).
4. Managers (stock price: options become more valuable as the stock price is driven up by repurchases).
5. Partial LBO (managers increase their percentage of ownership by not selling).
6. Exploit low stock price (the firm can buy low).
7. Optional dividend (the investor does not sell).

Stock Price Effect

The previous section implied that share repurchase will force the stock price to go up. Continue the basic example when the stock price immediately after repurchase was unchanged:

$$\text{New Price} = \frac{940{,}000}{9{,}400} = \$100.$$

Because we are assuming a firm that is in equilibrium, one year later the firm earns \$60,000 during the year and is again worth \$1,000,000 and the new share price after one year and with share repurchase at time zero is:

$$\text{New Price After One Year} = \frac{1{,}000{,}000}{9{,}400} = \$106.38.$$

Repeating the process (buying \$60,000 of shares and earning \$60,000 in the year) the stock price will increase every year. This price increase is not because the market likes the process but rather because the firm's value at the end of the year is constant and the number of shares decreases.

For the example, market cap $V = \$1,000,000$ and the amount used for share repurchase is Div $= \$60,000$ and the percentage of shares repurchased is p. For the example:

$$p = \frac{60,000}{1,000,000} = \frac{6}{100} \text{ or } 6\%$$

and 6% of the shares are being bought each year. The number of shares purchased each year will be decreased through time because the value per share increases.

The annual growth rate (g) in stock price is:

$$g = \frac{p}{1-p} = \frac{0.06}{0.94} = 0.06383$$

For the example, the stock price at time 0 was $100. One year later with share repurchase it was $106.38. This is a 0.0638 increase. The following table shows firm's projected price (remember, this is a firm that is not growing in a real sense).

Time Periods in Years	Stock Price ($g = 0.06383$)
0	$100.00
1	106.38
20	344.70
40	1,188.20

If instead of the stock price growing at 0.06383, assume the firm's stock price is only growing at 0.05.

Time Periods in Years	Stock Price ($g = 0.05$)
0	$100.00
1	105.00
20	265.33
40	704.00

Note that a little difference in assumed growth rates makes a large difference in expected future stock prices.

Summary

Share repurchase beats cash dividends if we only consider the after-tax consequences. Unfortunately, there is a tendency for investors to like cash dividends. The 2003 tax revision act of the U.S. lowered the tax rate on dividends to 0.15. This low tax rate encouraged corporations to pay (or increase) dividends and for investors to demand them. Unfortunately, investors do not necessarily benefit from the increased dividends since even the 0.15 tax on dividends might be larger in total than the total tax that would have taken place without the increase in dividend. In addition, there is the complexity of the alternative minimum tax that can substitute a 0.28 tax rate for the 0.15 tax. There are additional tax complications that may result in the tax rate on dividends not being equal to 0.15.

We have argued that for most firms (not all) share repurchase beats cash dividends. There are some investors who need a regular source of cash to pay their bills and are taxed at low rates or are not taxed. These investors want to buy common stock that are reliable dividend payors and hopefully where the dividend increases through time.

For the other investors, share repurchase by the corporation offers tax advantages over cash dividends. Assuming the firm has reasonable investment alternatives, retained earnings are a very reasonable alternative. Berkshire Hathaway (Warren Buffet's firm) is an excellent example of a firm that has profitably retained earnings even when it has not always had acceptable internal investments (it has invested in other firms).

Questions

1. Company A has 1,000,000 shares of common stock outstanding. The stock sells for $50 per share. The common stock pays $2 per share dividend (an annual payment).
   The market values the $2 dividend at $2,000,000.

   a. When the stock goes ex-dividend (the next buyer of the stock does not receive the dividend), the new stock price will be $_____.
   b. The investor owning 100 shares, taxed on dividends at 0.15, will have total wealth of $_____.

2. (Continue 1). The firm does not pay a dividend but it does buy back 40,000 shares at $50 per share.

   a. The new stock price, after repurchase, will be $_____.
   b. If the investor sells zero shares, the investor will have value of $_____.
   c. If the investor sells four shares, the investor will have value of $_____. The tax basis of the stock is $50 per share.
   d. (Continue c). Now assume the tax basis is $40. The investor will have value of $_____.

3. Assume a stock is selling at a price of $50. The company is buying back 0.04 of its stock each year.

   a. The expected price after one year is $_____.
   b. The expected price after five years is $_____.

Part III
Market Timing

The ability to market time is the most important skill an investor could possess. Unfortunately, it is a skill that is extremely rare, in fact it is very likely that no one has this skill.

Knowing that you, your friends, and your consultants do not have this skill is very important. If you sell at the right time and do not re-enter the market in a timely fashion, that can be worse than not having sold.

Chapter 10

The Stock Market Level

How can we tell when the stock market is too high or too low? We can readily admit that we cannot determine exactly when the level of the stock market is too high or too low. Anyone who had exact answers to the timing issue (when to buy and when to sell) would be immensely wealthy and would not be likely to write a book telling you how to do it. Anyone who is wealthy as a result of timing decisions is likely to be more lucky than clever. In this chapter, an effort will be made to identify some factors that can give insights into forming an opinion as to whether or not the stock market is at the right level. We observe that the business press does not do as good a job keeping the average investor as informed as it could do. Remember, the goal is to obtain objective information that will enable us to form an impression as to the reasonableness of the market's level.

The P/E Ratio

Define the P/E ratio to be the ratio of a firm's common stock price divided by the last 12 months earnings per share for that firm. Instead of one firm, the ratio can apply to a set of firms.

The first step is to obtain the average price earnings multiplier for the New York Stock Exchange firms, the Dow Jones Industrial Average firms, and Standard and Poors' 500. The second step is to obtain the multipliers for the firms listed on all the other major exchanges in the world.

There are two objectives. First, we want to determine whether the NYSE's multiplier is too high. Secondly, we recognize that the first conclusion is highly dependent on the investment alternatives. Thus, we have to compare the NYSE multiplier with the multipliers of the other major stock exchanges, as well as tracking the multiplier through time. Unfortunately, because of differences in accounting practices, the P/E ratios of different time periods (or for different countries) may not be comparable.

Currently, the P/E ratio of individual firms are supplied by the daily press but the average P/E for the market is only supplied sporadically. The market measure is needed to evaluate the level of the market.

When is a market's (or firm's) P/E too high? In the U.S., markets that have broken through 20 for their average P/E (as in 1929, 1987, and 2000) have collapsed so that the average P/E's are between 5 and 20. But in Japan, the market passed through 20 and went up to 70 and it has not gone back down to 20. The fact is that a P/E of 70 can be justified if the economy's growth rate is large enough or the alternative investments are bad enough.

Interest Rates and Dividend Yields

A second measure is to compare brokerage loan interest rates with average dividend yields. What is the net current cost of carrying an inventory of stocks? How is this cost changing through time?

In addition, we should compare interest rates on long-term bonds and dividend yields in order to measure the naive opportunity cost that exists (the comparison leaves out the capital gains potential of stock). While naive, the comparison is useful since it defines an opportunity cost that readily exists for investors, and the cost changes through time.

A variation of comparing interest rates and dividend yields would be to compare the average earnings price ratio (as a rough estimate of the cost of equity) with long-term bond yields.

Margin Loans

Tracking the amount of margin loans and the borrowing capacity of margin accounts through time would tell us something about the potential buying power of investors. It is interesting that the level of broker loans in 1929 is thought by many to have contributed to the 1929 to 1931 market crash but now it is next to impossible to find the information in the popular press (the Federal Reserve Bulletin does give some statistics). The total margin loans could be compared to the total capitalization of the market, but this is not a widely circulated number.

Cash-Stock Asset Allocation of Investors

The allocation between cash (or near cash) and stock being held by mutual funds, pension funds, and insurance companies would tell us a great deal about potential buying capacity. The balances in money funds and checking accounts of individuals would also be useful (as a measure of potential buying power).

International Comparisons

As we compare the P/E's of stock exchanges located in different countries it would be useful to know:

a. Significant differences in accounting conventions of listed firms in different countries.
b. Significant differences in financial practices (e.g., amount of debt leverage of the listed corporations).
c. Significant institutional and tax factors affecting investment decisions in stocks.
d. Inflation rates.
e. Purchasing power of the different currencies in their homeland (the cost of a market basket of like goods could be compared).

As investments across national boundaries become more common it will be increasingly important to supply enough information so that an investor is not making global investment decisions in the dark. Is a P/E of 75 for an exchange in Tokyo comparable to a P/E of 16 on the NYSE? If not, why?

Cash Flow Multiplier

In addition to the price earnings multiplier it would be useful to know the average cash flow from operations price multiplier for the different exchanges. This measure will tend to bypass the difficulties of interpretation arising from the fact that different accounting practices are being used. Instead of a cash flow multiplier, some analysts use earnings before interest, tax, depreciation and amortization (EBITDA).

Stock Index Measures

The stock index measures and their changes over time are of interest. Any peculiarities in the calculation of the indexes should be defined.

Book Value

The ratio of market value to book value of all listed stocks gives a measure of reasonableness. Again, we need to know any accounting peculiarities. Given the cost basis of accounting measures, we would expect the ratio to be larger than one, but would not expect it to be a large number (such as five) in a competitive economy with modest inflation.

The ratio of market value to book value of return regulated firms is of particular interest. A ratio greater than one is an indicator of overpricing of common stocks in the regulated industry.

Q Ratio

The ratio of replacement cost of an asset to the recorded cost is called Tobin's Q Ratio. If we divide the stock's market value by replacement cost of the firm's assets we get another useful measure. If the market value of the stock is four times larger than replacement cost, and if the historical norm is one, we might conclude that the market was tending to be too high.

Return on Investment and Return on Equity

The return on investment (income divided by total assets) and return on equity (income divided by the stockholders' equity) of the listed corporations are of interest as indicators of profitability. A 20% ROE is very good and a 5% ROE is not acceptable.

The ROI on replacement cost is also of interest (indicating the expected profitability of new investments).

These measures cannot be used (or amounts required defined) in an exact manner.

Macro Measures

The federal deficit and trade deficit are useful measures since they help indicate expected inflation and willingness (and ability) of foreign investors to buy stock.

The ratio of consumption to savings for the country is also an interesting macro measure.

Changes in the money supply are also of interest.

Almost Any Market Level Can Be Rationalized

Applying the most simple of discounted cash flow models we have for the expected P/E ratio:

$$P/E = \frac{\text{Dividend Payout Rate}}{\text{Stock Equity Discount Rate} - \text{Growth Rate}}$$

Assume a market where the observed P/E is 75, the retention rate is 0.9 and the required return for stockholders is 0.06. Firms are expected to earn a return on new investment of 0.06519. With these facts the implied growth rate is 0.9×0.06519 or 0.05867. The dividend payout rate is 0.1. The expected P/E is 75.

$$P/E = \frac{0.1}{0.06 - 0.05867} = 75$$

In this market a P/E of 75 is justified since 0.06519 is being earned incrementally on new investments and stockholders only require a return of 0.06. A change in the retention rate, the required return, or the return earned on new investments would lead to a change in the conclusion regarding the level of the market. For example, if the required return were 0.15 we would have:

$$P/E = \frac{1 - 0.9}{0.15 - 0.05867} = 1.09$$

The P/E will only be 1.09 given a required return of 0.15, a retention rate of 0.9, and an ability to earn only 0.06519 on new investments. The 0.06519 is much less than the 0.15 required return.

By making the "right" set of assumptions we can conclude that any market is not too high. The interpretation of any set of data regarding the level of the market will always involve some element of judgment.

Consequences of an Inflated Market

What happens to investors when a financial market is overpriced? We will consider the consequences of an overpriced stock market. To define what is meant by overpriced we will need to have two financial markets where one of them is overpriced compared to the other. It would be impossible to define a situation where all financial markets are overpriced. In the situation being described the second properly priced market sets an opportunity cost for capital funds invested in the overpriced market.

We will define an overpriced market to be a market where the investor earns a lower expected return for a given amount of risk than in a second market. In the real world it is extremely difficult to determine when a stock market is overpriced, except with the aid of hindsight.

Let us consider two markets. In the first market stocks are selling at a price earnings ratio of five. The following facts apply:

$$
\begin{aligned}
\text{dividend payout rate} &= 0.75 \\
\text{required return on stocks} &= 0.15 \\
\text{growth rate of stocks} &= 0
\end{aligned}
$$

Using a standard discounted cash flow dividend model, we determine the appropriate price earnings ratio to be 5:

$$
\frac{P}{E} = \frac{0.75}{0.15 - 0} = 5.
$$

In this market companies are retaining earnings, but no growth is expected. With this pessimistic forecast, the market should be willing to pay only five times earnings for the stock. If the observed price earnings ratio were 10, this market would be overpriced if the above information is accurate. The market becomes overpriced because it underestimates the cost of equity and/or overestimates the growth rate of dividends.

Now assume a second market where firms are retaining 0.9 of their earnings and the earnings are expected to grow at an annual rate of 0.149. We now determine the appropriate price earnings ratio to be 100:

$$
\frac{P}{E} = \frac{1 - 0.9}{0.150 - 0.149} = \frac{0.1}{0.001} = 100
$$

The 0.149 growth rate implies that with zero utilization of debt, a 0.9 retention rate, new investments will earn 0.166 (note that $0.9 \times 0.166 = 0.149$). We conclude that a P/E of 100 can be justified in this second market. It is not unreasonable to object to the above model and to the assumed inputs. For example, can we assume a 0.149 growth rate will continue forever? But if the above facts are accepted then a P/E of 100 is justified.

With the above inputs and accepting the dividend valuation model both markets are correctly priced if the P/E of the first is 5 and the second is 100. If the stock prices of the first market were to increase so that the P/E becomes ten, and if there are no other changes, then that market would be overpriced. Investors would only earn 0.075 in that market whereas they could earn 0.15 in the second market. The problem with evaluating the level of real stock markets is that we never know exactly the required return and the growth rate or the difference between the required return and the growth rate. If we assume a sufficiently high value for growth or a small value for the discount rate, we can justify any stock market level. It is only after the fact that hindsight enables us to know for sure that a market was overpriced.

The Investor in the Overpriced Market

Assume an investor can earn a risk adjusted expected return of 0.075 in the overpriced market and 0.15 in the properly priced second market. We will assume the overpriced market stays high but does not go higher.

First, consider a \$100 investment in the overpriced market, and after a year the investor earns \$7.50. The buying investor could have earned \$15 in the second market, thus has an annual opportunity cost of \$7.50. The \$100 investment changed nothing real for the investing group, considered as a group. However, the economic welfare of the individual investors has changed. The buying investor bails out the selling investor, and now owns an inferior investment. This inferior investment will result in an opportunity cost through time. The investor will earn 0.075 rather than 0.15.

While it is true that with a properly priced market the investor could have purchased the \$7.50 of income for a cost of $\frac{7.50}{0.15} = \$50.00$ rather than the cost of \$100, this transaction would have meant the current investor who sells would have lost \$50.00. The investors as a group who currently own the stock are trapped (unless a new customer can be attracted). A loss in value has already taken place, but it has not yet been taken note of by the players. There are no losses to the current holders of the stock who sell if the investor buys at the inflated price of \$100. The buying investor (or the holding investor) loses \$7.50 each year investing in the overpriced market, thus will have regrets if a correct analysis is made. After the sale, the selling investor has an opportunity to earn an extra \$7.50 per year by buying into the properly priced market.

If the market falls to \$50.00 (the present value of the cash flow stream) the investor holding during the fall has a \$50.00 capital loss. With a price of \$50.00 the capital loss will be equal to an implicit wealth transfer to the purchasing investor (who buys at \$50.00 rather than \$100) since that investor will pay \$50.00 less for the cash flow stream of the stock. The transactions for the investment group, where we consider the gains and losses to that entire group, can be described as a zero sum game.

Now assume that the $100 investment is a net addition to the market as when a company issues new common stock in the overpriced market to finance an investment that will only earn 0.075. At the end of the year the investor will have $107.50 instead of the $115 that could have been obtained in the alternative market. Now the country's economy is foregoing $7.50 of income per year because of the acceptance of an inferior real investment.

Thus, if the market stays high and if one investor merely replaces another investor, there is no net gain or loss to the economy. One person's loss is another person's gain. However, any buyer who holds the investment will lose through time. If the market stays high and there is a net addition to the market via the issue of common stock to finance a real investment, where the real investment only earns the market return or marginally above it, then there is an opportunity loss to the economy and the loss is compounded through time. The investors buying into the overpriced market at a cost of $100 will lose $7.50 in the first year and the loss will continue through time.

The transactions in the overpriced market are a zero sum game for the economy. A low return is earned but the cash flow resulting from the investment in the market is no different than if a lower level of stock prices existed. The flow of income to the investors is not affected by the level of the market, unless we consider what could have been earned by investing in the properly priced market. But remember, the entire set of investors cannot escape from the overpriced market without someone losing (but for every loss someone else will be better off). If there is a net real investment at the depressed return because of the low capital cost, then the economy incurs an opportunity cost by giving up the chance to earn a higher return in the second properly priced market.

Remember that stocks could have a lower expected return (before tax) than bonds but still be an acceptable investment opportunity given the several tax advantages of investing in stocks rather than bonds.

In summary, it is difficult to determine when the stock market is overpriced. If you think the market is overpriced, you should limit your purchases, but do not liquidate all your common stock investments since you do not know it is overpriced.

The Return Through Time

An investor in the overpriced market will lose through time. We again assume the overpriced market will give a 0.075 return and the properly priced market will give a 0.15 return. At the end of ten years for an investment of $100 we will have:

$$\text{Overpriced Market} \quad 100(1.075)^{10} = \$206$$
$$\text{Properly Priced Market} \quad 100(1.15)^{10} = \$405$$

There is a high cost ($199) to the investor of placing funds in the overpriced market. Because of the overpricing (the growth rate is lower than expected), a lower value will occur in ten years than is expected.

We could cause the values to be the same after ten years but this would require a change in the corporate earning rate or some type of price bubble in the overpriced market that would result in a speculative gain at time 10.

Net Consumers and Net Investors

Divide the investor group into two parts, net consumers and net investors. Net consumers are investors who are currently liquidating investments in order to consume part of their capital wealth. They want the market to be high to maximize their relative purchasing power when they sell.

The net investors are currently buying securities and adding to the amount they have invested in securities. All things equal they prefer for the market level to be low as they buy securities, and have it increase in value later (when they are ready to become net consumers).

Thus not all investors want the market level to increase and be overpriced. A significant percentage of investors (the investors who are net buyers) will prefer a fairly priced or an underpriced market. These investors should welcome a decrease in the value of the overpriced market, if the market is not still depressed when they start consuming.

If you are a net investor and the stock price goes up, you are not necessarily better off than if it had stayed constant or even gone down so that you could buy stocks at bargain prices.

The Investment Split

There is no one allocation that is correct. Only after the fact can we indicate the allocation that would have been correct.

But here is an allocation that you can use as the basis of your investment asset portfolio.

Cash and Equivalents	0.05
Tax Exempt Bonds	0.15 (depends on your tax bracket)
Diversified Stock	0.60
Stock in Company for which you Work	0.10
Bonds (in tax deferred account)	0.10

Assume that the above split is reasonable for a portfolio equal to $1,000,000. If the portfolio you manage is larger, the cash percentage can be reduced, the tax exempt bond percentage can be increased. Other percentages can be adjusted based on your risk preferences.

Investments in real estate investment trusts (REITs) are best executed in tax deferred accounts since REITs pay large dividends and thus are at a tax disadvantage compared to stocks.

Life-Cycle Funds

At the beginning of 2006, there were $49 billion invested in "life-cycle" funds and the amount invested was growing rapidly. These funds are split between stocks and bonds based on your age. The split is adjusted (less common stock) as you grow older. The investor receives both dividends and interest.

If you are 70 years old and have $10 million of investments, then it is reasonable for you to have 0.5 of your investments in safe fixed income securities. You do not need to be a clever stock picker to live comfortably for the next 30 years. With a zero investment return you would be able to spend $333,333 per year. If you earn 0.05 per year, you would have $500,000 to spend without reducing the size of your investment.

But suppose you are 70 years old and have $500,000 of savings. With conservative investments, you will soon run out of savings. You might as well try investments that can offer the possibility of 10–20% returns. This implies investments in common stocks.

The point is that if you manage the allocation of your portfolio, you can do a better job than a life-cycle fund that does not have all the personal financial information that you have. It is too easy for you to sell some stock and buy bonds to have the mix that is best for you. You do not need to buy a life-cycle fund that is aimed at an average person whereas you are unique.

If you do not have the knowledge or patience to adjust your portfolio consistent with your age and wealth, then buying a life-cycle fund might be a reasonable alternative. I would hope that a reader of this book would not need to have an investment in a life-cycle fund.

The "Number"

The search for the "number" continues. How much does a person need to have in a portfolio in order to retire and live comfortably for the remainder of his/her life?

I am not willing to estimate the "number". All of us have trade-offs between working and leisure time and between saving and consumption. Some of us have terrible jobs and we cannot wait for retirement. Others find their working environment to be enjoyable and would work for nothing (don't tell my boss).

Recognizing that we cannot determine the "number", I suggest you be conservative and take joy from saving a reasonable sum so that there is a small likelihood of having financial worries at retirement. Obviously, the above recommendation is vague, but it is the best I can do. Start saving early and accumulate a reasonable sum.

Needless to say, you do not want to incur costly debt. The traditional debt that is costly is credit card debt (costing 0.15 to over 0.20). The most important investment advice is avoid high cost debt. Consider the following table. Assume you borrow $1,000 at time 0 at a cost of 0.20 per year:

Years of Borrowing	Amount Owed
1	$1,200
5	2,480
10	6,192
20	38,338

Now assume you borrow $1,000 per year:

Years of Borrowing	Amount Owed
1	$1,200
5	8,929
10	31,150
20	224,020

If you borrow $1,000 a year for five years, at 0.20 you will owe $8,929 at time 5. You will pay $1,786 forever without reducing the amount you owe!

Forecasting

We would all like to be able to forecast the future. Unfortunately there will always be surprises. We must be able to deal with unexpected contingencies.

There are some things that we can successfully predict:

a. Labor will be relatively cheap in the far east (at least in the short run).
b. An invention or environmental change will make a commonly used product obsolete.
c. There will be labor unrest.
d. A new management style or technique will sweep the country.
e. An entrenched government will be voted out or thrown out in a revolution.
f. The stock market will reach a new high or low for the past _____ months.
g. The stock market will have its largest price increase (decrease) in one day.

Note that with each of the above forecasts, some highly relevant information is missing. Either the product, location, or date is lacking. Even a forecast of cheap labor in the far east requires a termination date.

Frequently, you can affect the future by taking an action today. But that does not eliminate the likelihood of future surprises. One way to survive as a forecaster is to forecast far enough in the future so that a bad forecast does not harm you today or tomorrow. Also, a diversification strategy is again recommended.

Summary

One reason why price bubbles have existed in the past is that the information available to investors has not been as good as it might have been. The problem of specifying the type of information that should be supplied to an investor in common stock is complicated by the fact that theory has not defined exactly how we determine that the stock market is too high or too low.

We know that the value of a stock is equal to the present value of its future dividends (where dividends are broadly defined to include any cash flow from firm to investor). But lacking the ability to forecast exactly future dividends, we must resort to other objective measures that help us reach a conclusion as to the level of the market. This section has suggested several measures that are objectively determined that could help an investor decide on the investment mix between stock and fixed claim, low risk assets.

The conclusion is that an overinflated market, even if it adjusts downward, does not necessarily hurt the overall economy. There can be redistributions of wealth within the investor group as well as outside it (a reduction in the stock market reduces the relative purchasing power of the investor group). Individual investors or groups of investors will, of course, be harmed. Some investors gained as the market went up and some investors lost as the market went down, but in sum the changes net out. It is a zero sum game for all investors, but there is a redistribution of wealth among different groups.

The portion of the investor group that is a net consumer prefers for the market to go up, even if it is overinflated before the increase. This group is a net seller of securities during the period in question and prefers to sell at the market peak. In like manner, the net investor group (the group is investing during the time period) prefers for the market level now to be low so it can buy at low prices, and later when it is net seller to sell at higher prices. Thus, there can be transfers of wealth between the different types of investors.

When there is a net addition to the investment amount (as when a corporation issues new common stock) and this investment promises to earn less than could be earned in a properly priced market, the investors as a group suffer an opportunity loss. The economy would have been better off with the funds invested in a properly priced market.

Changes in the stock market level may affect real investment decisions and the total amount of consumption by affecting the forecasts of managers and consumers. These real effects can be significant, thus we cannot conclude, without unreasonably bold assumptions, that changes in market level are of no real economic significance. But it is important to remove the misconceptions regarding market level or market risks so that attention can be focused on the real consequences of an overinflated market.

Looking carefully at her bank account
Widow Wiggens is astounded
As she sees her modest savings mount
When the interest is compounded.
Across the street her neighbor
Can only weep and fret.
She's overspent her credit cards —
Now faces lifelong debt.

The moral of this story is
Be sure you know the score
Before you borrow foolishly.
You could pay ten times more!
And if you wisely choose to save
You'll find that it is healthy
To insist on compound interest,
If you wish to end up wealthy.

Florence M. Kelso

Questions

1. Assume you borrow $10,000 and the interest rate on this loan is 0.20 (credit card debt frequently has interest rates of this magnitude). Determine the amount you owe after the following years:

Year	Amount Owed
1	
4	
30	
40	

2. Assume you borrow $10,000 per year (at the end of the year) and the interest rate on these loans is 0.20. Determine the amount you owe after the following years:

Year	Amount Owed
1	
10	
20	

Chapter 11

The Stock Market is Too High,
or Is It?

Question: In what year would you earn the highest annual return (54%) by investing in stocks?

Answer: For the answer, see the last page to this chapter.

Common Stock Equity

The Dow Jones Industrial Average is an index of the prices of 30 industrial stocks. The 30 firms included in the index change through time, but the index is widely accepted as a measure of the level of the stock market.

Over the past 100 years, the Dow Jones Industrial Average increased at an annual rate of about 5% (compounded). Add a 3% dividend yield and the stockholders earned about 8%. This was over a period that included two World Wars, many minor wars, and the great depression.

For any 20-year holding period since 1929, the common stock return is positive.

Long-term bonds beat common stock (on a before tax basis) for the following three 20-year holding periods (all involve the 1929 stock market crash):

1928 to 1947

1929 to 1948

1930 to 1949

Historically, stocks beat bonds. But is history a good predictor of the future? Because we cannot be sure of the future, we advocate diversification.

In doing your financial planning, I suggest assuming that you will earn 8% on your common stock investments. But do not be very surprised if you earn more or earn less.

For an optimistic scenario, you can assume a 10% return. The real (price level adjusted) return will be somewhat less.

Forecasting the Peaks

In 1928, the Dow Jones Industrial Index was at 300. It continued up in 1929 until the crash of October 1929. The index recovered some of its losses by December 1929, but then the depression struck and the index fell to 60 in 1932. In the 1970s, it broke through 1,000 and reached 2,169 in 1988 (1987 saw a temporary dip); by July 1997, it exceeded 8,000. In March 2006, the index was at 11,000.

From 1926–1999 an investment in the index earned an average return of slightly over 11%.

Some people can predict when the market tops out. In fact, it is said that any market price peak is forecasted at least ten times before someone gets it right. To make money, one must not only forecast the market peak and sell at the peak, but then one has to buy at or near the resulting bottom if one wants to brag about the investment strategy being implemented. Forecasting both the peak and deepest valley is very difficult.

One book popular in the year 2000 was *Irrational Exuberance* by Robert J. Shiller (published by Princeton University Press). He described a market that was too high in 1999 and he was mostly correct (the market fell in 2000). As of 2006, he has not yet published a second book saying "Now is the time to buy." One might conclude that it is not yet the time to buy, but given the alternatives, this is not obvious.

To highlight the difficulties of determining whether stocks are too high, we will consider 1929, the biggest stock market crash of all.

The Level of the Market: 1929

The classic stock market crash of 1929 is frequently cited as the prime example of the stock market bubble caused by excessive speculation that then burst. Were stock prices too high in 1929?

There is no question that the level of common stock prices increased in the 1920s to unprecedented highs. There is also no question that in October 1929 the boom ended and prices crashed and continued to fall until 1933. But these facts do not prove that stock prices were too high in 1929. It can be argued that they were too low in 1933.

Definition of Too High

When is a stock market too high? It is not because the market decreased in value or might decrease. The decrease might be unreasonable. A stock market is too high if an investment in an alternative financial security (possibly in a second market) will offer a higher return over the long term. Assume a \$100 investment in stock would lead to the value S_T at time T but an investment in bonds will lead to B_T and that B_T is larger than S_T for all values of T. With these facts, we can state that the stocks are selling at too high a level.

The above situation is the extreme example of a stock market bubble. What if the value of S_T is larger than B_T if the investment horizon is long enough (say 30 years)? While the definition of a stock market bubble becomes less precise as we allow S_T to be larger than B_T for some value of T, it is useful to define the bubble in terms of future relative values. It is important to recognize that a decrease in stock prices does not necessarily mean the stock prices were too high before the decrease.

Frequently, we see a real business downturn after a stock market price decline. It is difficult to determine if the market went down because the market was too high or went down because the market anticipated a decrease in business activity (and profits).

In 1929, stocks went down and in 1930 business activity slumped. In 2000, stock went down and the communications industry went into a bad slump, but other sectors of the economy took up the slack.

Were Stocks Obviously Overpriced in October 1929?

Economic Indicators were Strong

From 1925 to the third quarter of 1929, common stocks increased in value by 120% in four years, a compound annual growth of 21.8%. While this is a large rate of appreciation, it is not obvious proof of an "orgy of speculation." The decade of the 1920s was extremely prosperous and the stock market with its rising prices reflected this prosperity as well as the expectation that the prosperity would continue.

The fact that the stock market lost 90% of its value from 1929 to 1932 indicates that the market, at least using one criterion (actual performance of the market), was overvalued in 1929. John Kenneth Galbraith (1961) implies that there was a speculative orgy and that the crash was predictable: "Early in 1928, the nature of the boom changed. The mass escape into make-believe, so much a part of the true speculative orgy, started in earnest." Galbraith had no difficulty in 1961 identifying the end of the boom in 1929: "On the first of January of 1929, as a matter of probability, it was most likely that the boom would end before the year was out."

Compare this position with the fact that Irving Fisher (1930), one of the leading economists in the U.S. at the time, was heavily invested in stocks and was bullish before and after the October sell offs; he lost his entire wealth (including his house) before stocks started to recover. In England, John Maynard Keynes, possibly the world's leading economist during the first half of the 20th century, and an acknowledged master of practical finance, also lost heavily. Paul Samuelson (1979) quotes P. Sergeant Florence (another leading economist): "Keynes may have made his own fortune and that of King's College, but the investment trust of Keynes and Dennis Robertson managed to lose my fortune in 1929."

Galbraith's ability to 'forecast' the market turn is not shared by all. Samuelson (1979) admits that: "playing as I often do the experiment of studying price profiles with their dates concealed, I discovered that I would have been caught by the 1929 debacle." For many, the collapse from 1929 to 1933 was neither foreseeable nor inevitable.

The stock price increases leading to October 1929, were not driven solely by fools or speculators. There were also intelligent, knowledgeable investors who were buying or holding stocks in September and October 1929. Also, leading economists, both then and now, could neither anticipate nor explain the October 1929 decline of the market. Thus, the conviction that stocks were obviously overpriced is somewhat of a myth.

The nation's total real income rose from 1921 to 1923 by 10.5% per year, and from 1923 to 1929, it rose 3.4% per year. The 1920s were, in fact, a period of real growth and prosperity. For the period of 1923–1929, wholesale prices went down 0.9% per year, reflecting moderate stable growth in the money supply during a period of healthy real growth.

The financial fundamentals of the markets were also strong. During 1928, the price-earnings ratio for 45 industrial stocks increased from approximately 12 to approximately 14. It was over 15 in 1929 for industrials and then decreased to approximately 10 by the end of 1929. While not low, these price-earnings (P/E) ratios were by no means out of line historically. Values in this range would be considered reasonable by most market analysts today. For example, the P/E ratio of the S & P 500 in July 2003 reached a high of 33 and in May 2004 the high was 23.

To put the 1929 P/E ratios of 10 to 15 in perspective, note that government bonds in 1929 yielded 3.4%. Industrial bonds of investment grade were yielding 5.1%. Consider that an interest rate of 5.1% represents a $1/(0.051) = 19.6$ price-earnings ratio for debt. The stock prices and earnings were comparable to the debt returns.

J.W. Kendrick (1961) shows that the period 1919–1929 had an unusually high rate of change in total factor productivity. The annual rate of change of 5.3% for 1919–1929 for the manufacturing sector was more than twice the 2.5% rate of the second best period (1948–1953). Overall, the period 1919–1929 easily took first place for productivity increases, handily beating the six other time periods studied by Kendrick (all the periods studied were prior to 1961) with an annual productivity change measure of 3.7%. This was outstanding economic performance — performance which normally would justify stock market optimism.

In the first nine months of 1929, 1,436 firms announced increased dividends. In 1928, the number was only 955 and in 1927, it was 755. In September 1929, dividend increases were announced by 193 firms compared with 135 the year before. The financial news from corporations was very positive in September and October 1929.

The May 1929 issue of the *National City Bank of New York Newsletter* indicated the earnings statements for the first quarter of surveyed firms showed a 31% increase compared to the first quarter of 1928. The August issue showed that for 650 firms the increase for the first six months of 1929 compared to 1928 was 24.4%. In September, the results were expanded to 916 firms with a 27.4% increase. The earnings for the third quarter for 638 firms were calculated to be 14.1% larger than for 1928. This is evidence that the general level of business activity and reported profits were excellent at the end of September 1929 and the middle of October 1929. Article after article from January to October in business magazines carried news of outstanding economic performance.

To summarize: There was little hint of a severe weakness in the real economy in the months prior to October 1929. There is a great deal of evidence that in 1929 stock prices were not out of line with the real economics of the firms that had issued the stock. Leading economists were betting that common stocks in the fall of 1929 were a good buy. Conventional financial reports of corporations gave cause for optimism relative to the 1929 earnings of corporations. Price-earnings ratios, dividend amounts and changes in dividends, and earnings and changes in earnings all gave cause for stock price optimism.

If we take the Dow Jones high of September 1929 (386) and the 1929-year end value of 248.5, the market lost 36% of its value during that four-month period. Many of us, if we held stock in September 1929, would not have sold early in October. In fact, if I had money to invest, I would have purchased after the major break on Black Thursday, October 24. (I would have been sorry.)

What precipitated the October 1929 crash?

My research minimizes several candidates that are frequently cited by others (see Bierman, 1991, 1998, 1999, 2001, and 2004).

- The market did not fall just because it was too high — as argued above it is not obvious that it was too high.
- The actions of the Federal Reserve, while not always wise, cannot be directly identified with the October stock market crashes in an important way.
- The Smoot-Hawley tariff, while looming on the horizon, was not cited by the news sources in 1929 as a factor, and was probably not important to the October 1929 market. This tariff tended to make it more difficult for other countries to sell their products in the U.S.
- The Hatry Affair in England was not material for the New York Stock Exchange and the timing did not coincide with the October crashes. Hatry's firms went bankrupt and triggered a stock price decline in England. Hatry was sent to jail.
- Business activity news in October was generally good and there were very few hints of a coming depression.
- Short selling and bear raids were not large enough to move the entire market.
- Fraud and other illegal or immoral acts were not material, despite the attention they have received in later years.

Thursday, October 24, 1929

Thursday, October 24 (Black Thursday) was a 12,894,650 share day (the previous record was 8,246,742 shares on March 26, 1929) on the NYSE. The headline on page one of the *Times* (October 25) was "Treasury Officials Blame Speculation."

Tuesday, October 29, 1929

October 29 was "Black Tuesday." The headline the next day was "Stocks Collapse in 16,410,030 Share Day" (October 30, p. 1). Stocks lost nearly $16 billion in the month of October or 18% of the beginning of the month value. Twenty-nine public utilities (tabulated by the *New York Times*) lost $5.1 billion in the month, by far the largest loss of any of the industries listed by the *Times*.

An Interpretive Overview of Events and Issues

My interpretation of these events is that a statement by Snowden, England's Chancellor of the Exchequer, indicating the presence of a speculative orgy in America is likely to have triggered the October 3 break. Public utility stocks had been driven up by an explosion of investment trust formation and investing. The trusts, to a large extent, bought stock on margin with funds loaned not by banks but by "others." These funds were very sensitive to any market weakness. Public utility regulation was being reviewed by the Federal Trade Commission, New York City, New York State, and Massachusetts, and these reviews were watched by the other regulatory commissions and by investors. The sell-off of utility stocks from October 16 to October 23 weakened prices and created "margin selling" and withdrawal of capital by the nervous "other" money. Then on October 24, the selling panic accelerated.

The Public Utility Sector

In addition to investment trusts, intrinsic values are usually well defined for regulated public utilities. The general rule applied by regulatory authorities is to allow utilities to earn a "fair return" on an allowed rate base. The fair return is defined to be equal to a utility's weighted average cost of capital. There are several reasons why a public utility can earn more or less than a fair return, but the target set by the regulatory authority is the weighted average cost of capital.

In 1929, public utility stock prices were in excess of three times their book values.

Sooner or later this price bubble had to break unless the regulatory authorities were to decide to allow the utilities to earn more than a fair return, or an infinite stream of greater fools existed. The decision made by the Massachusetts Public Utility Commission in October 1929 applicable to the Edison Electric Illuminating Company of Boston made clear that neither of these improbable events were going to happen.

The utilities bubble did burst. Between the end of September and the end of November 1929, industrial stocks fell by 48%, railroads by 32% and utilities by 55% — thus utilities dropped the furthest from the highs. A comparison of the beginning of the year prices and the highest prices is also of interest: industrials rose by 20%, railroads by 19%, and utilities by 48%. The growth in value for utilities during the first nine months of 1929 was more than twice that of the other two groups.

The combination of an overpriced utility segment and investment trusts with a portion of the market that had purchased on margin appears to be a viable explanation of the crash. As of September 1, 1929 utility industry represented $14.8 billion of value or 18% of the value of the outstanding shares on the NYSE. Thus, they were a large sector, capable of exerting a powerful influence on the overall market.

Straws That Broke the Camel's Back?

Edison Electric of Boston

On August 2, 1929, the *New York Times* reported that the Directors of the Edison Electric Illuminating Company of Boston had called a meeting of stockholders to obtain authorization for a stock split. The stock went up to a high of $440. Its book value was $164 (the ratio of price to book value was 2.6, which was less than many other utilities).

On Saturday (October 12, p. 27) the *Times* reported that on Friday the Massachusetts Department of Public Utilities has rejected the stock split. The heading said "Bars Stock Split by Boston Edison. Criticizes Dividend Policy. Holds Rates Should Not Be Raised Until Company Can Reduce Charge for Electricity." Boston Edison lost 15 points for the day even though the decision was released after the Friday closing. The high for the year was $440 and the stock closed at $360 on Friday.

Conclusions and Lessons

Although no consensus has been reached on the causes of the 1929 stock market crash, the evidence cited above suggests that it may have been that the fear of speculation helped push the stock market to the brink of collapse. It is possible that President Hoover's aggressive campaign against speculation, helped by the overpriced public utilities hit by the

Massachusetts Public Utility Commission's decision and statements and the vulnerable margin investors, triggered the October selling panic and the consequences that followed.

An important first event may have been Lord Snowden's reference to the speculative orgy in America. The resulting decline in stock prices weakened margin positions. When several governmental bodies indicated that public utilities in the future were not going to be able to justify their market prices, the decreases in utility stock prices resulted in margin positions being further weakened resulting in general selling. At some stage, the selling panic started and the crash resulted.

What can we learn from the 1929 crash? There are many lessons, but a handful seem to be most applicable to today's stock market.

- There is a delicate balance between optimism and pessimism regarding the stock market. Statements and actions by government officials can affect the sensitivity of stock prices to events. Call a market overpriced often enough, and investors may begin to believe it.
- The fact that stocks can lose 40% of their value in a month and 90% over three years suggests the desirability of diversification (including assets other than stocks). Remember, some investors lose all of their investment when the market falls 40%.
- A levered investment portfolio amplifies the swings of the stock market. Some investment securities have leverage built into them (e.g., stocks of highly levered firms, options, and stock index futures).
- A series of presumably undramatic events may establish a setting for a wide price decline.
- A segment of the market can experience bad news and a price decline that infects the broader market. In 1929, it seems to have been public utilities. In 2000, high technology firms were candidates.
- Interpreting events and assigning blame is unreliable if there has not been an adequate passage of time and opportunity for reflection and analysis — and is difficult even with decades of hindsight.
- It is difficult to predict a major market turn with any degree of reliability. It is impressive that in September 1929, Roger Babson predicted the collapse of the stock market, but he had been predicting a collapse for many years. Also, even Babson recommended diversification and was against complete liquidation of stock investments (*Financial Chronicle*, September 7, 1929, p. 1505).

- Even a market that is not excessively high can collapse. Both market psychology and the underlying economics are relevant.

Answer to Question

In what year would you earn the highest annual return (54%) by investing in stocks?

The year is 1933, the depth of the great depression. When is it a good time to buy stocks?

References

Bierman, Harold, Jr. *The Great Myths of 1929 and the Lessons to be Learned.* Westport, CT: Greenwood Press (1991).

Bierman, Harold, Jr. *The Causes of the 1929 Stock Market Crash.* Westport, CT: Greenwood Press (1998).

Bierman, Harold, Jr. The Reasons Stock Crashed in 1929. *Journal of Investing* (1999), pp. 11–18.

Bierman, Harold, Jr. Bad Market Days, *World Economics* (2001), pp. 177–191.

Bierman, Harold. The 1929 Stock Market Crash. *EH.Net Encyclopedia*, edited by Robert Whaples (August 11, 2004). URL: http://eh.net/encyclopedia/article/Bierman.Crash.

Commercial and Financial Chronicle, 1929 issues.

Committee on Banking and Currency. *Hearings on Performance of the National and Federal Reserve Banking System.* Washington (1931).

Federal Reserve Bulletin, February, 1929.

Fisher, Irving . *The Stock Market Crash and After.* New York: Macmillan (1930).

Galbraith, John K. *The Great Crash, 1929.* Boston: Houghton Mifflin (1961).

Hoover, Herbert. *The Memoirs of Herbert Hoover.* New York: Macmillan (1952).

Ibbotson Associates, *2000 Yearbook*, p. 15.

Kendrick, John W. *Productivity Trends in the United States.* Princeton University Press (1961).

Moggridge, Donald. *The Collected Writings of John Maynard Keynes*, Volume XX. New York: Macmillan (1981).

New York Times, 1929 and 1930.

Samuelson, Paul A. Myths and Realities about the Crash and Depression. *Journal of Portfolio Management* (1979), p. 9.

Senate Committee on Banking and Currency. *Stock Exchange Practices.* Washington (1928).

Wall Street Journal, October 1929.

Washington Post, October 1929.

Wigmore, Barry A. *The Crash and Its Aftermath: A History of Securities Markets in the United States, 1929–1933.* Westport: Greenwood Press (1985).

Questions

1. Assume you successfully determine the right time to sell your stock portfolio because the market is overpriced.
   What is the problem?
2. Between the end of September and the end of November 1929, industrial stocks fell by 48%.
   Does this "prove" the market was too high?
3. The year 1933 was the year with the highest return to be earned (54%) by investing in stocks. What lesson does this impart?

Chapter 12

Ten Subordinate Rules
and Other Suggestions

This book opened with three basic rules for investing. You are about to be exposed to ten subordinate rules for investing in common stock. These rules are based on an objective of attaining a reasonable earnings level with reasonable risk. A different set of rules would be necessary if you wanted to become rich (and possibly poor). The rules are relatively conservative, but they are not the most conservative rules we could design. We could further reduce risk but would then suffer a reduction in expected return.

These rules are consistent with the three rules of Chapter 1 and are for an average investor. If you are not average, you should apply a scale factor. Later in the chapter, we will consider a non-average investor.

Rule 1: "Your Investment in Common Stock Should Reflect the Sum of Bank Deposits Plus Bonds Plus Insurance Plus Vested Pension Assets That You Own."

The objective of this rule is to have diversification in other investments than common stock. The limit of investment in stock is not scientifically derived but reflects the investor's risk preferences. Since all common stocks tend to move together (when the market is up, the returns of most stocks increase) there is a risk in being invested in common stock that cannot be diversified away by investing in other common stock. Thus a significant amount of your investment should be in other types of assets.

In 1929, a popular investment vehicle was the levered investment trust. The investment trust offered a large amount of diversification and a very high expected return. When the market crash occurred (1929 to 1932), the levered trust investors were wiped out. The stock market diversification was not sufficient given the amount of leverage. Other assets, relatively independent of the market and not financed with leverage, were needed to further reduce risk.

The allocation decision (the percentage invested in the stock market) is a major decision. Unfortunately, we are not able to offer much help in determining the optimum split between common stock and other assets. We do strongly recommend that the investment portfolio include other assets than stock so that the investor can survive the worst conceivable stock market fall in a comfortable fashion.

Rules 2 and 3 have as their objective the achievement of common stock diversification. No reasonable investment strategy wanting to limit risk can omit the objective of achieving an adequate level of diversification.

Rule 2: "Invest in Different Industries."

The objective is to insure diversification. If one buys shares in Exxon, Hess Oil, Phillips–Conoco, and Shell, all oil companies, there is less diversification achieved than buying shares in Exxon, IBM, Weyerheuser, and General Electric.

If one spreads the investment over ten different companies in ten different industries, then one will eliminate about 90% of the risk that can be eliminated by diversification in common stock.

Rule 3: "Rarely Buy Shares in the Company or the Industry for Which You Work (the Rule Does not Apply to Stock Options and Discount Purchases of Stock if There is no Restriction on the Sale of the Stock)."

The average person's major economic asset is his or her career. A worker's fortune is highly tied to that of the firm employing him (her). Risk should not be intensified by making additional discretionary investments in the same firm, unless the equity interests are being sold to you at bargain prices.

There are many stories that "prove" the above rule wrong. An executive of a small oil exploration company ignored the rule and became a millionaire. On the other hand, a junior level salesman of a mini-conglomerate followed the above advice and avoided losing his life's savings when the company went bankrupt. The employees of W.T. Grant were encouraged to invest heavily in the common stock of that company immediately before it went bankrupt.

Rule 4: "Your Tax Bracket and Status Should Influence the Mix of Investments. Use Simple Obvious Tax Shelters, but Beware of Sophisticated Devious Tax Shelters." Tax Exempt State and Local Bonds are an Example of an Obvious Tax Shelter for a High Tax Rate Individual.

Taxes are a very strong influence that should not be ignored in developing an investment strategy. The after-tax return, not the before tax yield, is the significant measure.

Frequently, sophisticated tax shelters offer relief from taxes, but there is likely to be a large amount of risk. Sometimes they are actually illegal. Complex tax shelters should receive a great deal of study before funds are committed. There are a large number of simple tax shelters that are relatively safe for a naïve investor.

Rule 5: "The Old Adage, 'Buy Low, Sell High,' is Wrong. Rarely Sell a Stock Voluntarily Unless You Need Cash, a Tax Loss, or Your Tax Situation has Changed." The Old Adage Should Read, "Buy Low and Hope the Stock Price Increases."

A tax loss occurs when securities that cost \$C are sold for less than \$C. The investor bought the securities expecting a capital gain but the price went down and there will be a tax loss when the securities are sold. A tax loss is needed by a taxpayer to balance capital gains or to create a deduction against ordinary income (a maximum of \$3,000 may be deducted against ordinary income).

One should not sell because the price has increased. Why pay a capital gains tax on the winnings? The fact that the stock price went up is not proof that the stock price is now too high. The price may be too high after the stock price has gone down and be too low after the stock price has gone up, but we do not know until the future becomes the present.

As the rule states, you might want to sell to realize a tax loss. Given both the tax on capital gains and the transaction costs, you do not want to sell just because a stock price has gone up. The new high price may be the low when looked at for the next ten years. Do not churn your portfolio. The market is relatively efficient, and for the practical purposes of an individual investor the market follows a random walk.

Rule 6: "Never Act on Advice (Tips) That Leads to Buying Without Your Checking on the Facts. If You are Adverse to Risk, You Might Listen to a Sell Tip, but Again the Recommendation is That You Check the Facts."

What is the source of the buy or sell recommendation? If it is an insider, the use of the information is likely to be illegal and unethical. If it is a broker, it is likely that you are receiving the information relatively late. Also, why does the broker arrive at the recommendation? What is the logic behind the recommendation?

Rule 7: "Do Some Basic Financial Analysis Before Buying or Selling Individual Stocks."

This is a somewhat controversial recommendation. It implies that the capital markets are not perfectly efficient and that it does some good (will increase the expected return) if one performs some basic financial analysis. Not all theoreticians would agree with the recommendation. They might argue that the stock prices rapidly reflect all publicly available information, and the average investor can just be a "price taker". If the market price is set in an efficient manner by the market forces, the individual investor can save the costs of analysis and just take any stock consistent with the diversification objectives.

The basic position of this book is that analysis has enough value to justify doing it before a buy or sell, but not enough value to justify a sale where there will be both transaction costs and capital gains taxes. Remember, for every person thinking it is time to sell, there is a buyer who thinks it is time to buy.

Rule 8: "Preferred Stock Yielding Less than an Equally Risk Rated Bond is not a Good Investment for a High Tax Investor or a Low Tax Investor."

The income from the bond described above is likely to be ordinary income and to be taxed as such. The return from investing in preferred stock may be ordinary income but may receive special tax treatment. Since the preferred stock is yielding less than the bonds, it is likely to be inferior to the bonds. Tax rate differentials could cause a modification in the conclusion.

Corporations have an edge in buying preferred stock because of the dividend received deduction that tends to make preferred stock a desirable investment for corporations. The same incentive does not exist for individuals to buy preferred stock. Preferred stock is not likely to be a good investment for individuals.

Rule 9: "Consider the Tax Consequences and the Fees Associated with Your Investment Strategy."

You want to consider the fees that are paid at the time of investment and that are paid through time. Unless you think that value is received for the fees being paid, choosing investment alternatives with lower fees is sensible. The level of fees is an important consideration as you do your financial planning.

Rule 10: "Follow the Spirit of the First Nine Rules, not the Letter."

It is difficult to write ten specific investment rules that are at all times applicable to all investors.

Modifications for a Non-Average Investor

A shift to non-average investors requires that we soften several of the above rules. We will consider the modifications for investors who have larger than average amounts to invest.

Rules 1, 2, 3, and 4 are all excessively restrictive for the non-average investor. For these four rules we will substitute:

> "Seek diversification: stocks and other investments. Buy many different stocks in different industries".

The objective of this rule is to achieve diversification which is the same objective as the four rules described earlier.

One rule that we would like to offer is:

> "Sell all common stock securities when the market is too high".

Unfortunately, we do not know how to implement this rule. If we were to offer this rule we should also inform you as to how you should determine that the market is too high. Lacking a test for determining that the market is too high, the rule is worthless. We can "feel" that the market is too high, but we do not "know" that it is too high. The market can always go higher, thus a sell strategy can lead to regret.

The same difficulty applies to determining that the market is too low and now is the time to buy. The market may be lower than it was, but we do not know that it will not go lower. Forecasting turns in the market trend is an art, not a science.

Some investors try to forecast market turns. They sell when the market is too high (and thus will fall) and buy when the market is too low (and thus will rise). Implementing this strategy so that the investor's position is improved is very difficult. In the Spring of 1987, the author thought the market was too high and sold a large percentage of the stock he held. In October, the market fell proving the author to be correct. But this neglects two considerations. First, the market continued up after the sale (which was not at the peak). Secondly, it was not possible (because of restrictions on pension fund investing) to buy back the stock after October. All things considered, the successful forecast that the market was too high in the Spring of 1987 cost the author money.

We can generalize the above experience. For market timing to be profitable, it is not sufficient to forecast correctly that the market is too high. We have to be correct that the market will not go higher and if it does fall, we have to buy back in before the prices rise and wipe out the gains resulting from having sold. Given the transaction costs, taxes, and lost gains while out of the market, it is difficult to make profits from market timing (someone you know will do it successfully but do not bet they will be correct for the next set of changes).

One of the major factors affecting the results (returns) from investing is the percentage of the portfolio invested in common stock. Not having a significant common stock allocation can be the most significant investment strategy error.

Investment Decisions

What type of vehicles? The choices include:

a. Stock (individual stocks, mutual funds, exchange-traded funds)
b. Debt (short versus long term; tax exempt versus taxed)
c. Hybrids (convertible bonds and preferred stock)

d. Hedge funds
e. Private equity
f. Real estate
g. Exotics (stamps, coins, art, quilts, etc.)

Hedge funds and private equity are both types of investments that require considerable knowledge and wealth. Knowledge is required about the people who will be administering the money you invest. Unless you know well the people involved, you should not invest. Secondly, it is necessary that the funds invested be a small part of your investment portfolio so that you can still have diversification. The same warnings apply to the investment in exotics, and in addition you should have some reasonable degree of expertise before you buy a material amount.

Real estate investing carries the same types of warnings, but if you buy into publicly traded real estate investment trusts (REITs), we can relax the constraints. A REIT investment is much like investing in common stock with a large dividend. Because of the large dividend, a REIT investment is best placed in a tax deferred account, unless you want cash.

Very Short-Term Investments

Cash and near cash investments yield very low returns, but all investors want some degree of liquidity. The alternatives are:

a. Savings account (pass-book account)
b. Checking account (the balance might reduce fees)
c. Money market account (offered by brokerage firms, banks, and mutual funds)
d. Brokerage accounts
e. Certificates of deposit (offered by banks) offer the best yield of the accounts listed but your capital is tied up for a committed time period.

You should get interest rate quotes and compare the rates with the restrictions. The rates change through time thus there is no one recommendation good for all time periods.

In 2006, a three-month CD yielded slightly over 2%, a Money Market Fund between 2.5% and 4%. An aggressive Money Market Fund could yield slightly above 4%. Very short-term investments are sensible for liquidity purposes but not for long-term investment purposes.

Tax Considerations

The leading investment candidates for a taxed account are:

- Common Stock
- Hedge Funds (maybe if you are rich and an expert investor)
- Private Equity (same qualifications as for Hedge Funds)
- Real Estate (direct purchases)

Common stock and real estate lose some of their tax advantages in a tax deferral account.

The leading investment candidates for tax deferral accounts (IRA, Roth, Pensions, Keough, 401 K, etc.) are:

- Debt
- Hybrids (convertible debt)
- Common stock (if the amount invested in taxed accounts is not large enough)

Uncertainty

The future returns for the following investment alternatives are relatively uncertain:

- Stocks
- Hybrids (convertible debt)
- Hedge Funds
- Private Equity
- Real Estate
- Exotics
- High-yield Debt

Investment grade debt is relatively certain, but uncertainty is increased the longer the life of the debt.

Transaction Costs

The following have very high transaction costs:

- Hedge Funds
- Private Equity
- Exotics (stamps, art, coins, etc.)

The following have relatively low transaction costs (buying and selling):

- Stock (especially index funds and exchange-traded funds, ETFs)
- Debt
- Hybrids (convertible debt)
- Real Estate (is not easily classified)

Expertise Required

The following require a high level of expertise:

- Stocks (buying individual stocks especially low rated and international securities)
- Hedge Funds
- Private Equity
- Debt (junk)
- Exotics

The following do not require a high level of expertise:

- Stock (index funds, exchange-traded-funds, mutual funds)
- Debt (investment grade)
- Hybrids (investment grade)
- Real Estate (a diversified and market-traded REIT)

Increasing the Risk

How can an investor lose 100% of an investment when the market falls 10%? Consider the following investment strategies.

a. Buy stock on margin (use borrowed funds). For example, an investor has $100, borrows $900 and buys $1,000 of stock. The market goes down 10% so that the investment is worth $900. The investor is wiped out.
b. Do not diversify. The market is down 10% but the one stock you bought is the stock of a now bankrupt firm whose stock is worthless.
c. Buy call options. These became worthless after 90 days when the stock did not go up.
d. Sell puts. Had to pay the owner of the puts when the stocks went down to zero.

Strategies That Can Lead to Maximum Returns (and Maximum Losses)

1. Buy one "best" stock; do not diversify.
2. Buy one "best" call option; this implicitly uses leverage.
3. Buy stock market index futures.
4. Use debt to do any of the above.
5. Invest in a mutual fund that uses a large amount of leverage.
6. Sell "puts" (and have stocks go down (and lose) or go up (and win)).
7. Own no stocks (and have stocks go down and stay down and win). Or have stocks go up and lose big.

Using margin debt to finance stocks adds to risk. In 2006, the margin interest rate was 5% to 10% with the lower rate given to investors who borrowed a large amount (over $500,000).

Inflation Protection

Inflation can erode the value of a conventional investment. The financial community, including the Federal Government offer securities that offer inflation protection.

TIPS

TIPS are Treasury Inflation Protected Securities issued by the U.S. Treasury. The rate of return of the TIPS is indexed to the consumer price index (principal grows with inflation). The interest paid increases with inflation. There is reasonable liquidity since several brokerage firms trade them. Firms selling TIPS funds include:

- Fidelity (no sales charge; expenses max at 0.5% of assets)
- Vanguard
- Pimco

The issue price of a TIP is $1,000. The additions to principal because of inflation result in a federal income tax but the gain is not taxed at the state or city level. Interest is paid-semiannually. The life of a TIP can be as long as 20 years.

Example

Assume the TIP has a base annual rate of 2%. Inflation is 5% for six months. Tax rate is 0.34.

New principal	$1,050 ($1,000 plus 5%)
Six months interest	0.01
Interest	$10.50 (six months)

Taxable income:

Principal increase	50.00
Interest	10.50
Taxable income	$60.50
Tax $(0.34) =$	$20.57

Corporate Inflation Bond

Corporations also issue inflation bonds. While there are many types of bonds, typically interest rate is adjusted monthly and interest is paid monthly (interest could be adjusted and paid every six months). For example, with 0.01 basic interest and 0.05 inflation, we have for six months interest:

$$\text{Six months rate} = 0.01 + 0.05 = 0.06.$$
$$\text{Interest for six months } 0.06(1,000) = \$60.$$

With a 0.34 tax rate, the tax is:

$$\text{Tax} = \$20.40 \text{ (also state and local)}$$

and the

$$\text{Net cash flow} = \$39.60$$

We previously showed for the TIPS with the same facts:

$$\text{Net cash flow for TIPS} = 10.50 - 20.57 = -\$10.07$$

With no further inflation:

Principal payment at maturity: Corporate bond $= \$1,000$
Principal payment at maturity: TIPS $= \$1,050$

Corporate inflation bonds have been issued with maturities of 5, 7, or 10 years. The bond characteristics are likely to change.

Long-Term Financial Planning and Setting Goals

Financial Planning

a. There is a trade-off between incremental consumption now, consumption later, or leaving wealth for heirs.
b. Allocating savings between types of assets.

This book offers a large amount of advice on the trade-off between consumption now and consumption later. Consider the following lesson regarding the power of compound interest. Assume a 0.10 annual interest rate. If a person saves $100 a year for ten years, the savings will be $1,594 after ten years. That person can then spend $159.40 a year forever! In like manner, borrowing $100 a year for ten years will result in paying $159.40 a year and never reducing the debt.

Setting Goals

a. The minimum amounts needed for life's predictable crises (or challenges) should be estimated.
b. Amounts in excess of the minimums needed should depend on circumstances.

The minimum amount is difficult to define. Set reasonable goals.

Investing Strategies

First Line of Defense

Earn money while you can and control consumption consistent with savings goals.

Before Investing in Securities

Buy a residence (buying offers tax advantages).
Have adequate insurance if you have a family.
You need working capital (cash).

Multiple Choice

Investors have a wide range of choices and this book cannot do justice to the array of alternatives, but consider the following:

Money market funds (invested in short-term debt)
  Expense ratio 0.34 to 0.50%
Bond funds (U.S. corporations and U.S. Government)
  Expense ratio 0.39 to 0.80%
Bond funds international (predominantly foreign corporations and governments)
  Expense ratio 0.90 to 1.0%
Real estate funds (rental income and capital appreciation)
  Expense ratio 0.50 to 0.90%
Growth and income funds: domestic or international
  Expense ratio 0.10 to 1.20%
Growth funds — international
  Expense ratio 0.90 to 2.03%

You can buy a large range of international area "growth funds". For example, you can choose funds that specialize in Canada, China, Emerging Markets, Europe, Japan, Latin America, Nordic, Southeast Asia, Worldwide,

By choosing a range of mutual funds you can gain worldwide diversification without trying to choose the specific companies that are going to be winners and even more importantly, which stocks of which companies are going to be winners.

Index funds (collections of common stocks) are designed to track the performance of price indices for market sectors by industry or by geography (e.g., Asia, Latin America, Europe, etc.). The index funds are good alternatives since they offer a large amount of diversification at very low cost (some as low or lower than 0.10% of assets managed).

Stock index funds have relatively low expenses. In 2006, the industry average (depending on the nature of the index) was as low as 0.25% of the value of the assets managed to 0.44% (for the Total Market Index). But Fidelity charged only 0.07% for "eligible customers". Fidelity has many funds where the expense ratio approaches or is less than 1.00%.

Let us assume a reasonable amount of diversification of the common stock investment. It is also desirable to diversify into other types of assets, e.g., bonds, munis, real estate, and TIPs.

While we want to reduce risk, it is not possible to eliminate risk. For example, one could buy 90-day U.S. Treasury bills. In 90 days, they will convert into cash. The two main risks with this riskless security are that when reinvested they will earn a very low return and secondly they lose purchasing power because of surprise inflation.

Tuesday through Sunday many newspapers carry stock market quotations. For each stock listed, there are numbers giving the high-low for the year, daily volume, P/E ratio, dividend yield, high, low and closing for the previous day and the change in price for the previous day.

Lifestyle Fund

Lifestyle funds own a percentage of their investment in stocks and bonds. In one buy order the investor buys both stocks and bonds and achieves more diversification than with a typical stock mutual fund (with only stocks).

This type of fund is sensible for the investor who finds it psychologically impossible to buy bonds otherwise. The alternative is to cure oneself of the phobia against buying bonds.

Of course the objection to a high tax individual owning taxable bonds in a taxed account still holds. The lifestyle fund should be lodged in a tax deferral account.

A Brief History of the Dow Jones Industrial Average

In 1932, the Dow closed at 59.93. It first reached 1,000 in November 1972 and when it reached 6,500 in December 1997, Alan Greenspan talked of "irrational exuberance". The market did collapse in 2000, but by 2006 it was above 12,000.

If you had sold at 6,500 in response to Greenspan's implicit warning that the market was too high, you would have lost out on a 70% price increase (plus cash dividends) paid out during the period 1998 to 2006, an eight-year period.

My Favorite Book on Investments

My favorite book on investing is *Where Are the Customers' Yachts?* by Fred Schwed, Jr.[1] The title is derived from an "ancient story" (p. XIII).

---

[1]Schwed, Fred, Jr., *Where Are the Customers' Yachts?*, New York: Simon and Schuster (1940, 1955).

A broker was showing a naïve visitor around New York's financial district. He pointed out yachts owned by famous bankers and brokers. The visitor asked, "Where Are the Customers' Yachts?"

Summary

Do not be greedy. Do not feel "comfortable" with the stock market or expect to get rich. A greedy strategy leads to inadequate diversification and an excessive amount of churning. The book is strongly against both of these actions.

Your investment strategy is a function of your season of life. Specific decisions must be tailor-made. The reader of a book such as this is likely to reject a majority of the above rules for himself (herself), but accept them for one's heirs. For ourselves the rules are too conservative, and we "know" that we can do better than an investor will do by following the rules of this book. On the other hand, we know our children do not possess our intuitive insights into the market and if they gamble with their inheritance (or with their earned savings) they will lose all. Thus this book is aimed at winning a few converts in a subtle manner. You might even realize that some of the rules have application to your affairs.

Above we offered ten investment rules that are basically a conservative investment strategy. If followed in approximate fashion by the readers of this book, they, on the average, will tend to earn the same return as the market return. Individual readers may do a bit better and a bit worse than the market but if more than ten different securities in different industries are purchased it will be difficult to beat the market by a great deal (or to lose by much). One thing is certain, the recommended strategy will lead to savings in taxes and transaction costs compared to more active investment strategies.

Unfortunately, the recommended strategies cannot match the appeal of those investment evangelists who know how to beat the market. These believers can tell you when the market is too high and you should convert to cash, when one should be completely in gold and when one should sell gold. They can even pick out the individual stocks which are going to beat the market and then tell you when to sell. They cannot only do this for you, but they can do it for millions of other followers of their wisdoms. Or can they?

The ten rules for an average investor can be condensed to five summarized by:

DAMET

where

D stands for diversification

A stands for analysis

M stands for market turns that most of us cannot predict profitably

E stands for efficient markets (relatively), meaning that we should not churn

T stands for taxes. The choices must take taxes into consideration

Following the recommendations of this book you give up the luxury of hoping that the investment prophets can forecast the future and make you rich.

It is fun to invest $1 and win $1,000,000. If two million people invest $1 each and if one person wins $1,000,000 and everyone else loses their investment, this is not an attractive investment (it is an unfair gamble) for all the investors except the winner. The fact that one person becomes very happy does not mean that engaging in the gamble is to be recommended. Unfortunately, we do not know of any gambles in the real world where a small investment has a large probability of winning a very large dollar amount with a small probability of loss. We can follow a strategy where a relatively small investment can have a small probability of a large gain, and the investment can even be a fair gamble. But there will be a large probability of winning nothing or even a large probability of losing a significant amount of the investment.

It would be nice if we could promise more. But to promise more would be dishonest and misleading. Be satisfied that there is available an easily attained financial strategy that is within your grasp that is likely to lead to a reasonable positive expected return.

Consider the following thought of John Maynard Keynes (the leading economist of the 20th century):

> "I have reluctantly reached the conclusion that nothing is more suicidal than a rational investment policy in an irrational world."

John Maynard Keynes

After the October 1929 market crash, Keynes thought it (November) was a good time to buy common stock. He was wrong. He was not well diversified in investments beyond the stock market.

We conclude with a little something from my favorite poet.

> After reading this text
> I have a sad hunch
> The author is saying
> There's just no free lunch.

Florence M. Kelso

Questions

1. Assume a corporation has a 70% dividend received deduction for stock
   dividends. Only 30% of the dividend is subject to the 0.35 corporate tax.
   Assume a preferred stock has a dividend yield (before tax) of 0.10. A
   bond yields 0.09.

   Which security promises the higher after-tax return?

2. Assume the stock market is too high and it is expected to decrease in
   value over the next period. Cash dividends are 0.25 of market value.
   Dividends are taxed at 0.15.

   The investor can invest in a money market fund and expect to earn
   0.025. Ordinary income is taxed at 0.35.

   What do you recommend?

Solutions to End of Chapter Questions

Solutions: Chapter 1

1. To achieve diversification:

   a. Buy a wide range of stocks

      Different firms in an industry
      Different industries
      Different geographical areas
      Different sized firms

   b. Buy other assets

      Cash and equivalent
      Tax exempt bonds
      Government bonds (Federal)
      Industrial bonds

   c. Real assets

      Real estate
      Other real assets

2. A gambling casino (the expected value is negative for the customers).

3. a. $8
   b. $8(1 - 0.35) = 5.20
   c. $8(1 - 0.65) = 2.80
   d. $8(1 - 0.15) = 6.80

4. All investments have some risk. The safest investment has the risk that an alternative investment might do better.

Solutions: Chapter 2

1. $FV = 100(1.10)^3 = \$133.10$
   or
   $FV = 100(1.10)(1.10)(1.10) = \$133.10$

2. $PV = 133.10(1.10)^{-3} = \$100$
   or
   $$PV = \frac{133.10}{1.10(1.10)(1.10)} = \$100$$

3. Expected Return $= \dfrac{6+2}{50} = \dfrac{8}{50} = 0.16$

4. Dividend Yield $= \dfrac{2}{50} = 0.04$ or 4%

5.

	Time 0	**Time 1**	**IRR**
	$-1,000$	$+1,150$	
Debt	$+800$	-864	
	-200	286	0.43

6. $(1-t)0.10 = 0.06$
   $1 - t = 0.6$
   $t = 0.40$ A tax rate of 0.4 or larger.

Solutions: Chapter 3

1. Expected value $= 0.3(1{,}000) - 200 = \$100$

   It is a fair gamble since the expected value is positive.

2. Percentage Reduction $= \dfrac{n-1}{n} = \dfrac{9}{10} = 0.9.$

   The variance will be 10,000.

3. a.

$50 \times 0.5 =$	25
$30 \times 0.5 =$	15
Expected Value $=$	40

   b.

$(50-40)^2 0.5 =$	50
$(30-40)^2 0.5 =$	50
Variance	100

   c. Standard deviation $= 10$

4. A large variance but less risky (\$50 and \$30) are larger than (\$30 and \$20).

Solutions: Chapter 4

1. $PV = 1{,}000(1.10)^{-2} = \dfrac{1{,}000}{1.21} = \$826.45$

2. $PV = 1{,}000(1.20)^{-2} = \$694.44$

3. Bond value goes down.

4. $\text{Return} = \dfrac{10 + 2}{40} = \dfrac{12}{40} = 0.30$

5. $PV = \dfrac{50 + 2}{1.12} = \$46.43$

   All things equal, buy.

6. John K. Earns $= 0.10 - 0.05 - 0.02 = 0.03$.

Solutions: Chapter 5

1. Stock Value $= \dfrac{5}{0.15 - 0.10} = \dfrac{5}{0.05} = \$100$

2. Stock Value $= \dfrac{5}{0.15 - 0.14} = \dfrac{5}{0.01} = \$500$

3. Stock Value $= \dfrac{5}{0.15 - 0.05} = \dfrac{5}{0.10} = \$50$

4. P/E Ratios (E = \$20)

    For Problem 1:   P/E = 5
    For Problem 2:   P/E = 25
    For Problem 3:   P/E = 2.5

5. Seller Lost $20 - 4 = \$16$.

6. Required Expected Return $= 0.05 + (0.09 - 0.05)1 = 0.09$.

7. Seller Lost $35 - 4 = \$31$.

Solutions: Chapter 6

1. a. Quick Ratio $= \dfrac{5{,}000 + 3{,}000}{10{,}000} = 0.8$

   b. Current Ratio $= \dfrac{20{,}000}{10{,}000} = 2$

2. Ratio $= \dfrac{30{,}000}{15{,}000} = 2$

   Can pay the debt in two years with operating flows. This is optimistic since the cash flow will have other uses.

   Ratio $= \dfrac{30{,}000 - 8{,}000}{15{,}000} = \dfrac{22{,}000}{15{,}000} = 1.47$

   If the cash and accounts receivable were used to reduce debt, the pay down period would only be 1.47 years.

3. a. P/E $= \dfrac{450{,}000}{50{,}000} = 9$ times

   b. Ratio of Current Price to EBITDA $= \dfrac{450{,}000}{100{,}000} = 4.5$ times

Solutions: Chapter 7

1. Bond "P/E" $= \dfrac{1}{0.05} = 20$ or $\dfrac{1,000}{50} = 20$

   Stock P/E $= \dfrac{40}{2} = 20$

   There is a tie.
   The bond is likely to be safer.
   The stock price may be growing.

2. Bonds yield (after tax) $= 0.06(1 - 0.35) = 0.039$
   Dividend yield $= k$
   $$k(1 - 0.15) = 0.039$$
   $$k = 0.0459$$

3. $k_i(1 - 0.35) = 0.0425$
   $k_i = 0.0654$

4. A $100 Dividend
   The $100 is taxed and the investor nets $65.

   $FV = 65(1.10) = \$71.50$

   A $100 Retention
   $FV = 100(1.12)(1 - 0.35) = \$72.80$
   Retention is preferred.

5. Yes. The 0.12 is taxed; it is reasonable that the investor only earns 0.10 after tax.

Solutions: Chapter 8

1.

	0	1
Borrow	+1,000	−1,060
Investment	−1,000	+1,100
Taxes Saving	+350	
Taxes Paid (1,100)0.35		−385
	+350	−345

The cost of borrowing the $350 is negative. Yes, this is desirable.

2. Tax Deferral

	0	1	
Investment	−1,000	+1,100	
Tax Saving	+350		
Earnings (0.085)	−350	+379.75	
Taxes		−385	
	−1,000	+1,105.25	0.10525
Taxed Account			
	−1,000	+1,085	0.085

Tax deferral wins.

3. Time

0	10,000
1	10,000
2	10,000

$$\text{Time 2 Value} = 10{,}000 + 10{,}000(1.2) + 10{,}000(1.2)^2$$
$$= 10{,}000 + 12{,}000 + 14{,}400 = \$36{,}400.$$

4. $FV = 36{,}400(1.2) + 10{,}000 = \$53{,}680$

5. $53{,}680(0.20) = \$10{,}736.$

Solutions: Chapter 9

1. a. $50 - 2 = \$48$ per share

   or

   $$\frac{50{,}000000 - 2{,}000000}{1{,}000{,}000} = \$48$$

   b. Initial value $= 100(50) = \$5{,}000$.

Dividend	$200
Tax (0.15)	-30
Stock value	4,800
	$4,970

2. a. $\text{Price} = \dfrac{50{,}000000 - 2{,}000000}{1{,}000000 - 40{,}000} = \dfrac{48{,}000000}{960{,}000} = \$50$

   b. Value $= 100(50) = \$5{,}000$

   c. Value $= 50(96) + 4(50) = 4{,}800 + 200 = \$5{,}000$

   d. Value $= 50(96) + 4(50) - 4(50 - 40)0.15$
   $= 1{,}000 - 6 = \$994$
   where the capital gain is $4(50 - 40) = \$40$ and the capital gains tax is $0.15(40) = \$6$.

3. $g = \dfrac{p}{1 - p} = \dfrac{0.04}{0.96} = 0.04167$
   p at Time $1 = 50(1.04167) = \$52.083$
   p at Time $5 = 50(1.04167)^5 = \$61.32$

Solutions: Chapter 10

1.

Year	Amount Owed
1	$12,000
4	20,734
30	2,373,763
40	14,697,715

2.

Year	Amount Owed
1	$10,000
10	259,587
20	1,866,880

Solutions: Chapter 11

1. You have to determine when is the right time to buy.
2. In a sense, yes. But if the market anticipated the depression that was about to start the fall in stock prices are reasonable.

   The September 1, 1929 level was reasonable if business activity did not decrease significantly.
3. 1933 was a terrible year for the profitability of U.S. corporations.

   It is very difficult to determine when to buy unless you are using history.

Solutions: Chapter 12

1. Assume a $1,000 investment.

Preferred stock yields		$100
Taxable income	$30	
Tax rate	0.35	10.50
After-Tax Return		$89.50
Bond yields		$90.00
Tax (0.35)		31.50
After-Tax Return		$58.50

or for preferred stock

$$0.10(1 - 0.3(0.35)) = 0.10(1 - 0.105) = 0.0895$$

For debt:

$$0.09(1 - 0.35) = 0.0585$$

2. Stock return:

$$0.025(1 - 0.15) = 0.02125$$

Bond return:

$$0.025(1 - 0.35) = 0.01625.$$

The stock investment wins.

Glossary

Accumulation Factor $= (1 + r)^n$. See Compound Interest.

After-Tax Yield $= (1 - \text{marginal tax rate})(\text{interest rate of taxable securities})$.

Annual Return: The amount earned on a security (or securities) over a 12-month period.

Annuity: Equal payments for a defined time period; may be for a lifetime.

Assets: Items of value owned by a firm purchased or obtained in an economic transaction.

Average Value: Expected Value.

Balance Sheet: A presentation of assets that equals the sources of those assets (liabilities and stockholders' equity).

Beta Factor: Measure of systematic risk or volatility caused by market changes. It is the percentage change in return expected for a given percentage change in market return.

Bond: Also referred to as debt — contractual obligation of a debtor to pay interest (if any) and principle at maturity.

Book Value of a Stock $=$ Total assets minus liabilities of a firm divided by number of shares outstanding.

Book Value Per Share $= \dfrac{\text{Value of the common stock equity}}{\text{Total number of common stocks outstanding}}$.

Brokerage Account: An investor's account with a brokerage firm.

Buying on the Margin: The investor uses a loan from a broker to finance part of the purchase price of securities.

Call Option: A contact giving the right to buy a defined number of shares of common stock at a given exercise price on or before a given date.

Call Premium: Call price minus face value; the price at which the bond can be called in excess of its face value.

Capital Asset Pricing Model (CAPM): (See Beta Factor) — A market pricing model. Assumes only systematic risk is relevant in setting market price.

Capital Market (Wall Street): The collection of all investors (buyers and sellers of securities).

Capital Structure: Amount of debt plus the amount of stock equity of a firm. A ratio of debt to equity may be computed.

Cash Flow: The changes in the bank account associated with a transaction.

$$\text{Cash Flow Multiplier} = \frac{\text{Price of stock}}{\text{Cash flow per share}}.$$

Clean Surplus Rule: No accounting entries bypass the income statement.

Common Stock: A security issued by a corporation indicating ownership in that corporation.

Compound Interest: The interest earned on interest. The formula for future value is:

$$(1 + r)^n$$

where r = annual interest rate and n = number of years.

Conversion Premium: For a convertible bond, the excess of the face value of the bond over the bond's conversion value. The initial conversion premium is:

$$\frac{\text{Face value of debt} - \text{Value if converted into common stock}}{\text{Value if converted}}$$

where value if converted is equal to stock price times number of shares the bond will be converted into.

Convertible Bond: A bond that is convertible (at the investor's decision) into common stock.

Corporate Bond: A bond (debt) issued by a corporation.

Cost of Equity Capital: Annual return required by investors to invest in a firm's stock.

Covariance: The relationship of two variables defined mathematically:

$$\text{Covariance} = E(x - \bar{x})(y - \bar{y}).$$

$$\text{Current Ratio} = \frac{\text{Current assets}}{\text{Current liabilities}}.$$

Debt: A firm's capital that includes a legal obligation to pay that includes bank loans, notes, bonds, leasing of equipment, etc.

$$\text{Debt-Equity Ratio} = \frac{\text{Total debt}}{\text{Total assets}} \text{ of a firm.}$$

Debt to Total Capitalization Ratio

$$= \frac{\text{Debt}}{\text{Debt} + \text{Stockholders' equity}} \text{ of a firm.}$$

Deep Discount Bond: A bond selling at much less than face value.

Discount Rate: Interest rate used in computing the present value of a future cash flow. Cost of equity capital used by investors to value a common stock is a discount rate.

Diversify: Investing in wide range of assets or securities; in different industries; in different geographical areas.

$$\text{Dividend Price Multiplier} = \frac{\text{Price of stock}}{\text{Dividends}}.$$

Dividend Yield: Dividend earned in a single year divided by the stock price of a share of stock.

Dollar Averaging: A defined fixed amount invested in each time period in a given stock.

EBITDA: Earnings before interest, taxes, depreciation and amortization.

Efficient Market Theory: Market price rapidly reflects all publicly available information.

Equity: Either common or preferred stock of a firm.

Exchange-Traded Funds (E.T.Fs): Baskets of securities of an industry, geographical area, etc., that can be purchased as a unit.

Expected Return

$$= \frac{(\text{Future value of stock minus price of stock}) \text{ plus future dividend}}{\text{Price of stock}}.$$

Expected Return

$$= \text{Risk-free return}$$
$$+(\text{market's expected return} - \text{risk-free return}) \text{ Beta.}$$

Expected Value: Sum of the products of probability of each outcome times the cash flow of each outcome; also called "average" or "mean value".

Expense Ratio of a Fund: Annual expenses of a fund divided by assets of the fund.

Face Value of a Bond: The maturity value of a bond.

Fair Gamble: A gamble (or an investment) with a positive expected value.

Federal Government Security: A debt security issued by the U.S. Government and backed by the U.S. Government.

Financial Subsidiary: A finance corporation owned by an operating company.

401(K): A tax deferred savings account for retirement; the amounts invested in a 401(K) have not been taxed. They will be taxed when taken out of the account as will the interest earned.

Funds of Funds: A fund that invests in a set of diversified funds.

Future Benefits of Common Stock: Dividend plus future stock price.

FutureValue

$$= \text{Price}(1 + \text{return on investment})^{\text{years invested}} \text{ assuming a zero tax rate.}$$

Growth Rate of Dividend: The annual rate of dividend growth for a stock. A function of retention rate and earnings opportunities for firm.

Hedge Fund: An organization (not regulated) that obtains and invests capital from rich, well informed investors.

$$\text{Income-Asset Ratio} = \frac{\text{Income before interest}}{\text{Average of assets}} = \text{ROI}.$$

Income Statement: Reports the period's income (revenue minus expenses) of the firm.

$$\text{Income-Stock Equity Ratio} = \frac{\text{Income}}{\text{Average of stockholders' equity}} = \text{ROE}.$$

Index Fund: An investment fund that tracks a market index; it is likely to be a low cost investment vehicle.

Leverage: The use of debt; leads to more risk.

Liabilities: Debts; amounts that are legal obligations by the corporation or individual.

Life-Cycle Fund: Funds split between stocks and bonds based on the investor's age.

Lifestyle Fund: A mutual fund that includes both stocks and bonds.

Liquidity: Cash, or near cash assets, readily available for spending; another measure of liquidity is $\dfrac{\text{Total debt} - \text{Current assets}}{\text{Funds from operations}}$. This measure considers the flows into the firm.

Marginal Dollar of Income: The next dollar of income.

Marginal Tax: The tax on the next dollar of income.

Margin Purchase: Buying a security from a broker with borrowed funds.

Market Index: An index of stock prices, e.g., Dow Jones Industrial Average.

Market Portfolio: Best of the set of efficient portfolios.

Mean Value: See "Expected Value".

Measures of Liquidity:

(1) quick ratio $= \dfrac{\text{Liquid assets}}{\text{Current liabilities}}$

(2) current ratio $= \dfrac{\text{Current assets}}{\text{Current liabilities}}$. Also see "Liquidity".

Money Market Account: A fund invested in short-term securities so money is readily available for investor.

Mutual Fund: An entity established by an investment corporation to enable investors to achieve extensive diversification and "expert" investment management.

Negatively Correlated Investments: When one investment goes up in value the other investment goes down in value.

Net Investor: A person currently buying securities.

Net Working Capital $=$ Current assets minus current liabilities.

Par Value: A number assigned to a share of common stock that has legal significance, but no direct economic significance.

Portfolio: A collection (set) of securities (stocks, bonds, etc.).

Portfolio Variance: See "Variance".

Preferred Stock: Preferred stock dividends must be paid before any common stock dividend is paid, but the dividends are not a legal obligation before they are declared. Less secure than a bond. More secure than a common stock.

Premium Over Bond Value: The percentage of value of a convertible bond in excess of the value of a convertible as straight debt $= \dfrac{\text{Market value now} - \text{Value of comparable straight debt}}{\text{Value of comparable straight debt}}$.

Present Value (PV): The value today of a cash flow to be received at a specific future date.

Present Value $= (1 + r)^{-n} \times$ estimate of future cash flow, where $r =$ annual interest rate and $n =$ number of years.

Present Value Factor (see Present Value): The amount by which you multiply the future cash flow to determine the present value of the cash flow: $(1 + r)^{-n}$.

Price Earning Multiplier (P/E ratio) $= \dfrac{\text{Stock value per share}}{\text{Earnings per share}}$.

Price Equity Ratio (P/E) $= \dfrac{\text{Price of stock}}{\text{Earnings}}$.

Private Equity: Privately owned business; the stock is not publicly traded; an investment fund that finances corporations, takes them private, and after a period of years generally takes them public.

Put Option: The right of the owner to sell at a given price to the seller of the put until an expiration date.

Random Walk Theory: One cannot tell future stock prices by looking at their past prices.

Rate of Return: Percentage earned compounded over entire life of asset. More exactly this is the "internal rate of return".

Real Estate Investment Trust (REIT): A real estate investment vehicle that has specific dividend and taxation aspects.

Reinvestment by Corporation: The firm's income minus the amount of dividend payment and is retained by the firm to be invested in the firm.

Reserve Accounts: An entry made to the right-hand side of the balance sheet for unusual items where a liability might occur.

Return on Investment (ROI)

$$= \frac{\text{Expected price change on asset} + \text{Dividend}}{\text{Price now}}$$

$$\text{or} \quad \frac{\text{Income}}{\text{Beginning of period investment}}.$$

Returns from Investment: Income realized from a security.

Risk Reduction $= \dfrac{N-1}{N}$ achieved by investing the same amount in N different securities ($N =$ number of different securities held; all securities have the same variance and the same correlation coefficient).

ROE: Stock equity income divided by stock equity; return on equity.

ROI: $\dfrac{\text{Income}}{\text{Assets}} =$ Return on Investment.

Roth 401(K): A form of savings account for retirement; the amounts invested in a Roth 401(K) have been taxed — the interest earned in the Roth 401(K) will never be taxed if the specified conditions are satisfied. This alternative may or may not be available, depending on the tax law.

Standard Deviation: Square root of the variance.

Stockholders' Equity: A firm's assets minus liabilities.

Stockholders' Equity/Asset Ratio $= \dfrac{\text{Stockholders' equity}}{\text{Total assets}}.$

Stockholders' Equity/Debt Ratio $= \dfrac{\text{Stockholders' equity}}{\text{Total debt}}.$

Stock Index: A measure of the value of a specific collection of stocks over time.

Stock Market Index Futures: A security whose value is tied to the stock market index.

Stock Value $= \dfrac{\text{Next period's cash dividends}}{\text{Cost of equity capital} - \text{Growth rate in dividend}}$

There are other methods of valuation. This method assumes dividends grow at a constant rate for perpetuity.

Stop Order: The broker is directed to sell the stock if the stock price drops to a given stock price.

Systematic Risk: The amount a stock changes in value as the market level changes.

Tax Profile: The expected tax status of the tax payer.

Tobin's Q Ratio: Ratio of replacement cost of an asset to the recorded cost; James Tobin, a Nobel prize winner, was the author of this widely used ratio.

Treasury Inflation Protected Securities (TIPS): Issued by the U.S. Government; offers protection from inflation.

Unfair Gamble: A gamble (or an investment) with a negative expected value.

Unsystematic Risk: All risks of price changes not caused by the market changes.

Variable Annuity: The payments to the owner depend on the performance of an investment portfolio.

Variance: One measure of risk of a portfolio (the larger the variance, the greater the risk).

Variance = (Outcome − Expected value)^2 × (Probability of the outcome) added over all outcomes.

Working Capital: Current assets. Net working capital equals current assets minus current liabilities.

Zero Coupon Bond: Only pays interest at maturity, and before maturity sells at a discount to maturity value.

Index